HEALTH CARE ISSUES, COSTS AND ACCESS

MEDICARE PART B

PREMIUMS AND HIGH-EXPENDITURE DRUGS

HEALTH CARE ISSUES, COSTS AND ACCESS

Additional books in this series can be found on Nova's website under the Series tab.

Additional E-books in this series can be found on Nova's website under the E-book tab.

HEALTH CARE ISSUES, COSTS AND ACCESS

MEDICARE PART B

PREMIUMS AND HIGH-EXPENDITURE DRUGS

RICARDO VISSER
EDITOR

nova publishers
New York

For permission to use material from this book please contact us:
Telephone 631-231-7269; Fax 631-231-8175
Web Site: http://www.novapublishers.com

Library of Congress Cataloging-in-Publication Data

ISBN: 978-1-62808-097-1

Published by Nova Science Publishers, Inc. †New York

CONTENTS

Preface		**vii**
Chapter 1	Medicare: Part B Premiums *Patricia A. Davis*	**1**
Chapter 2	Medicare: High-Expenditure Part B Drugs *United States Government Accountability Office*	**45**
Chapter 3	Medicare Primer *Patricia A. Davis, Scott R. Talaga, Cliff Binder, Jim Hahn, Suzanne M. Kirchhoff, Paulette C. Morgan and Sibyl Tilson*	**83**
Index		**127**

PREFACE

Medicare is a federal insurance program that pays for covered health care services of most individuals aged 65 and over and certain disabled persons. In 2013, the program is expected to cover 52 million persons (43 million aged and 9 million disabled) at a total cost of $598 billion. Most individuals (or their spouses) who are 65 and older, and have worked in covered employment and paid Medicare payroll taxes for 40 quarters receive premium-free Medicare Part A (hospital insurance). Those entitled to Medicare Part A (regardless of whether they are eligible for premium-free Part A), have the option of enrolling in Part B, which covers such things as physician and outpatient services and medical equipment. This book provides an overview of Medicare Part B premiums and high-expenditure drugs, with a focus on eligibility and enrollment.

Chapter 1 – Medicare is a federal insurance program that pays for covered health care services of most individuals aged 65 and over and certain disabled persons. In 2013, the program is expected to cover 52 million persons (43 million aged and 9 million disabled) at a total cost of $598 billion. Most individuals (or their spouses) who are 65 and older, and have worked in covered employment and paid Medicare payroll taxes for 40 quarters receive premium-free Medicare Part A (Hospital Insurance). Those entitled to Medicare Part A (regardless of whether they are eligible for premium-free Part A), have the option of enrolling in Part B, which covers such things as physician and outpatient services and medical equipment. Beneficiaries have a seven-month initial enrollment period, but those who enroll in Part B after their initial enrollment period and/or reenroll after a termination of coverage may be subject to a "delayed enrollment penalty" which is equal to a 10% surcharge for each 12 months of delay in enrollment and/or reenrollment.

Under certain conditions, select beneficiaries are exempt from the delayed enrollment penalty; these include working individuals (and their spouses) with group coverage, some military retirees, and some international volunteers. While Part A is financed primarily by payroll taxes paid by current workers, Part B is financed through a combination of beneficiary premiums and federal general revenues. The standard Part B premiums are set to cover 25% of projected per capita Part B program costs for the aged, with federal general revenues accounting for the remaining amount. In general, if projected Part B costs increase or decrease, the premium rises or falls proportionately. Most Part B participants must pay monthly premiums, which do not vary with a beneficiary's age, health status or place of residence. However, since 2007, higher-income enrollees pay higher premiums to cover a higher percentage of Part B costs. Premiums of those receiving benefits through Social Security are deducted from their monthly payments. Additionally, certain low-income beneficiaries may qualify for Medicare cost-sharing and/or premium assistance from Medicaid through a Medicare Savings Program. The Social Security Act includes a provision that holds most Social Security beneficiaries harmless for increases in the Medicare Part B premium; affected beneficiaries' Part B premiums are reduced to ensure that their Social Security checks do not decline from one year to the next. Each year, the Centers for Medicare & Medicaid Services (CMS) determines the Medicare Part B premiums for the following year. The standard monthly Part B premium for 2013 is $104.90. Higher-income beneficiaries, currently defined as those with incomes over $85,000 a year, or couples with incomes over $170,000 per year, pay $146.90, $209.80, $272.70, or $335.70 per month, depending on their income levels. Current issues related to the Part B premium that may come before Congress include the amount of the premium and the rate of increase in recent years (and the potential net impact on Social Security benefits), modifications to the late enrollment penalty, and possible increases in Medicare premiums as a means to reduce federal spending and deficits.

Chapter 2 – In 2010, the Medicare program and its beneficiaries spent about $19.5 billion on Part B drugs—drugs that are commonly administered by a physician or under a physician's close supervision in physicians' offices and hospital outpatient departments. Some of these drugs are particularly expensive for Medicare, either because they are used by a large number of beneficiaries or because their prices are high. These drugs generally differ from drugs beneficiaries obtain through Medicare Part D, which are usually self-administered and for which Medicare, its beneficiaries, and the states spent $61.7 billion in 2010.

Chapter 3 – Medicare is a federal program that pays for covered health care services of qualified beneficiaries. It was established in 1965 under Title XVIII of the Social Security Act to provide health insurance to individuals 65 and older, and has been expanded over the years to include permanently disabled individuals under 65. Medicare, which consists of four parts (A-D), covers hospitalizations, physician services, prescription drugs, skilled nursing facility care, home health visits, and hospice care, among other services. Generally, individuals are eligible for Medicare if they or their spouse worked for at least 40 quarters in Medicare-covered employment, are 65 years old, and are a citizen or permanent resident of the United States. Individuals may also qualify for coverage if they are a younger person with a permanent disability, have End-Stage Renal disease (permanent kidney failure requiring dialysis or transplant), or have amyotrophic lateral sclerosis (ALS, Lou Gehrig's disease). The program is administered by the Centers for Medicare & Medicaid Services (CMS), and by private entities that contract with CMS to provide claims processing, auditing, and quality oversight services. In FY2013, the program will cover approximately 52 million persons (43 million aged and 9 million disabled) at a total cost of about $598 billion. Spending under the program (except for a portion of administrative costs) is considered mandatory spending and is not subject to the appropriations process. Services provided under Parts A and B (also referred to as "traditional Medicare") are generally paid directly by the government on a "fee-for-service" basis, using different prospective payment systems or fee schedules. Under Parts C and D, private insurers are paid a monthly "capitated" amount to provide enrollees with at least a minimum standard benefit. Medicare is required to pay for all covered services provided to eligible persons, so long as specific criteria are met. Since 1965, the Medicare program has undergone considerable change. For example, during the 111th Congress, the Patient Protection and Affordable Care Act (ACA; P.L. 111-148 and P.L. 111- 152) made numerous changes to the Medicare program that modify provider reimbursements, provide incentives to increase the quality and efficiency of care, and enhance certain Medicare benefits. However, in the absence of further congressional action, the Medicare program is expected to be unsustainable in the long run. The Hospital Insurance (Part A) trust fund has been estimated to become insolvent in 2024. Additionally, although the Supplementary Medical Insurance (Parts B and D) trust fund is financed in large part through federal general revenues and cannot become insolvent, associated spending growth is expected to put increasing strains on the country's competing priorities. As such, Medicare is expected to be a high-priority issue in the 113th Congress, and Congress may consider a variety of Medicare reform options ranging from further modifications of provider payment mechanisms to redesigning the entire program.

In: Medicare Part B
Editor: Ricardo Visser
ISBN: 978-1-62808-097-1

Chapter 1

MEDICARE: PART B PREMIUMS*

Patricia A. Davis

SUMMARY

Medicare is a federal insurance program that pays for covered health care services of most individuals aged 65 and over and certain disabled persons. In 2013, the program is expected to cover 52 million persons (43 million aged and 9 million disabled) at a total cost of $598 billion. Most individuals (or their spouses) who are 65 and older, and have worked in covered employment and paid Medicare payroll taxes for 40 quarters receive premium-free Medicare Part A (Hospital Insurance). Those entitled to Medicare Part A (regardless of whether they are eligible for premium-free Part A), have the option of enrolling in Part B, which covers such things as physician and outpatient services and medical equipment.

Beneficiaries have a seven-month initial enrollment period, but those who enroll in Part B after their initial enrollment period and/or reenroll after a termination of coverage may be subject to a "delayed enrollment penalty" which is equal to a 10% surcharge for each 12 months of delay in enrollment and/or reenrollment. Under certain conditions, select beneficiaries are exempt from the delayed enrollment penalty; these include working individuals (and their spouses) with group coverage, some military retirees, and some international volunteers.

* This is an edited, reformatted and augmented version of Congressional Research Service, Publication No. R40082, dated April 5, 2013.

While Part A is financed primarily by payroll taxes paid by current workers, Part B is financed through a combination of beneficiary premiums and federal general revenues. The standard Part B premiums are set to cover 25% of projected per capita Part B program costs for the aged, with federal general revenues accounting for the remaining amount. In general, if projected Part B costs increase or decrease, the premium rises or falls proportionately.

Most Part B participants must pay monthly premiums, which do not vary with a beneficiary's age, health status or place of residence. However, since 2007, higher-income enrollees pay higher premiums to cover a higher percentage of Part B costs. Premiums of those receiving benefits through Social Security are deducted from their monthly payments. Additionally, certain low-income beneficiaries may qualify for Medicare cost-sharing and/or premium assistance from Medicaid through a Medicare Savings Program. The Social Security Act includes a provision that holds most Social Security beneficiaries harmless for increases in the Medicare Part B premium; affected beneficiaries' Part B premiums are reduced to ensure that their Social Security checks do not decline from one year to the next.

Each year, the Centers for Medicare & Medicaid Services (CMS) determines the Medicare Part B premiums for the following year. The standard monthly Part B premium for 2013 is $104.90. Higher-income beneficiaries, currently defined as those with incomes over $85,000 a year, or couples with incomes over $170,000 per year, pay $146.90, $209.80, $272.70, or $335.70 per month, depending on their income levels.

Current issues related to the Part B premium that may come before Congress include the amount of the premium and the rate of increase in recent years (and the potential net impact on Social Security benefits), modifications to the late enrollment penalty, and possible increases in Medicare premiums as a means to reduce federal spending and deficits.

INTRODUCTION

Medicare is a federal insurance program that pays for covered health care services of most individuals aged 65 and over and certain disabled persons. Medicare serves approximately one in six Americans and virtually all of the population aged 65 and over. In calendar year (CY)2013, the program is expected to cover 52 million persons (43 million aged and 9 million disabled) at a total cost of $598 billion, accounting for approximately 3.6% of GDP.[1] The Medicare program is administered by the Centers for Medicare & Medicaid Services (CMS).

Medicare consists of four parts—Parts A through D. Part A covers hospital services, skilled nursing facility services, home health visits, and hospice services. Part B covers a broad range of medical services and supplies, including physician services, laboratory services, durable medical equipment, and outpatient hospital services. Enrollment in Part B is voluntary, however most beneficiaries (about 93%) with Part A also enroll in Part B. Part C provides private plan options, such as managed care, for beneficiaries who are enrolled in both Parts A and B. Part D provides optional outpatient prescription drug coverage.[2]

Each part of Medicare is funded differently.[3] Part A is financed primarily through payroll taxes imposed on current workers (2.9% of earnings, shared equally between employers and workers) which is credited to the Hospital Insurance (HI) Trust Fund, and beneficiaries generally do not pay premiums for Part A. In 2013, total Part A expenditures are expected to reach $280 billion representing about 47% of program costs. Parts B and D, the voluntary portions, are funded through the Supplementary Medical Insurance (SMI) Trust Fund which is financed primarily by general revenues (transfers from the Treasury) and premiums paid by enrollees. In 2013, about $2.7 billion in fees on manufacturers and importers of brand-name prescription drugs will also be used to supplement the SMI trust fund.[4] In 2013, Part B expenditures are expected to reach about $239 billion and Part D expenditures, about $70 billion, representing 40% and 13% of program costs respectively. (Part C is financed proportionately through the HI and SMI Trust Funds.)

Part B beneficiary premiums are set at a rate each year equal to 25% of expected per capita Part B program costs for the aged for the year.[5] In 2013, most beneficiaries pay the standard monthly Part B premium of $104.90.[6] Higher-income enrollees pay higher premiums set to cover a higher percentage of Part B costs,[7] while those with low incomes may qualify for premium assistance through one of several Medicare Savings Programs administered by Medicaid. Individuals who receive Social Security or Railroad Retirement Board retirement or disability benefits have their Part B premiums automatically deducted from their benefit checks. Part B premiums are generally announced in the fall prior to the year that they are in effect (for example, the 2013 Part B premiums were announced in November 2012).[8]

In addition to premiums, Part B beneficiaries must also pay other out-of-pocket costs when they use services. The annual deductible for Part B services is $147 in 2013. After the annual deductible is met, beneficiaries are responsible for coinsurance costs, which are generally 20% of Medicare-approved Part B expenses.

This report provides an overview of Medicare Part B premiums, including information on: Part B eligibility and enrollment; late enrollment penalties; collection of premiums; determination of annual premium amounts; premiums for high-income enrollees; premium assistance for low-income enrollees; protections for Social Security recipients from rising Part B premiums; and, historical Medicare Part B premium trends. This report also provides a summary of various premium related issues that may be of interest to Congress. Specific Medicare and Social Security publications and other resources for beneficiaries, and those who provide assistance to them, are cited where appropriate.

MEDICARE PART B ELIGIBILITY AND ENROLLMENT

An individual (or the spouse of an individual) who has worked in covered employment and paid Medicare payroll taxes for 40 quarters is entitled to receive premium-free Medicare Part A benefits upon turning 65. Those who have paid in for fewer than 40 quarters, may enroll in Medicare Part A by paying a premium.[9] All persons entitled to Part A (regardless of whether they are eligible for premium-free Part A) are also entitled to enroll in Part B. An aged person not entitled to Part A may enroll in Part B if he or she is age 65 or over and either a U.S. citizen, or an alien lawfully admitted for permanent residence, who has resided in the United States continuously for the immediately preceding five years. Those who are receiving Social Security or Railroad Retirement Board (RRB) benefits are automatically enrolled in Medicare, and coverage begins the first day of the month they turn 65.[10] These individuals will receive a Medicare card and a "Welcome to Medicare" package about three months before their 65th birthday.[11] Those who are automatically enrolled in Medicare Part A are also automatically enrolled in Part B.[12] However, because beneficiaries must pay a premium for Part B coverage, they have the option of turning it down.[13] Disabled persons who have received cash payments for 24 months under the Social Security or RRB disability programs also automatically receive a Medicare card and are enrolled in Part B unless they specifically decline such coverage.[14] Those who choose to receive coverage through a Medicare Advantage plan (Part C) must enroll in Part B. Persons who are not receiving Social Security or RRB benefits, for example because they are still working or have not yet reached their full retirement benefit eligibility age,[15] must file an application with the Social Security Administration or RRB for Medicare benefits.[16] There are two kinds of enrollment periods, one that occurs when individuals are initially eligible for Medicare, and the later an annual general enrollment period for those who missed signing up during their initial enrollment period. A beneficiary may drop Part B enrollment and re-enroll an unlimited number of times, however premium penalties may be incurred.

Initial Enrollment Periods

Those who are not automatically enrolled in Medicare may sign up during a certain period when they first become eligible. The *initial enrollment* period is seven months long and begins three months before the month in which the individual first turns 65. (See Table 1.)

Table 1. Initial Enrollment Period
Month of Enrollment and Effective Dates

	3 months before the month one turns 65	The month during which one turns 65	Up to 3 months after the month one turns 65
Effective Dates	If one signs up during the first 3 months of one's initial enrollment period, Part B coverage starts the 1st day of one's birthday month.[a]	If one enrolls during one's birthday month, the start date will be the 1st day of the next month.	The start date will be delayed if one enrolls during the last 3 months of the initial enrollment period. • If one signs up in the month after the month one turns 65, coverage starts 2 months after enrollment. • If one signs up 2 or 3 months after the month one turns 65, coverage starts 3 months after enrollment.
Example for someone turning 65 during the month of June The 7 month initial enrollment period would run from March 1st through September 30th.	If one enrolls in March, April, or May, coverage begins June 1st.	If one enrolls in June, coverage begins July 1st.	• If one enrolls in July, coverage begins September 1st. • If one enrolls in August, coverage begins November 1st. • If one enrolls in September, coverage begins December 1st.

Source: SSA Publication No. 05-10043.

[a] If one's birthday falls on the 1st of the month, then the enrollment period starts a month earlier and coverage may begin on the 1st day of the month prior to one's birthday month.

Beneficiaries who do not file an application for Medicare benefits during their initial enrollment period could be subject to the Part B delayed enrollment penalty (see "Late-Enrollment Premium Penalty and Exceptions" below). If an individual accepts the automatic enrollment in Medicare Part B, or enrolls in Medicare Part B during the first three months of the initial enrollment period, coverage will start with the month in which an individual is first eligible, e.g., the month of the individual's 65th birthday. Those who enroll during the last four months, will have their coverage start date delayed from one to three months after enrollment.[17] The initial enrollment period of those eligible for Medicare based on disability or permanent kidney failure is linked to the date the disability or treatment began.[18]

General Enrollment Period

An individual who does not sign up for Medicare during the initial enrollment period must wait until the next *general enrollment* period. In addition, persons who decline Part B coverage when first eligible, or terminate Part B coverage, must also wait until the next general enrollment period to enroll or re-enroll. The general enrollment period lasts for three months from January 1st to March 31st of each year, with coverage beginning on July 1st of that year. A delayed enrollment penalty may apply.[19]

LATE-ENROLLMENT PREMIUM PENALTY AND EXCEPTIONS

Beneficiaries who enroll in Part B after their initial enrollment period and/or reenroll after a termination of coverage may be subject to a "delayed enrollment penalty." In 2011, about 1.3% of Part B enrollees (about 600,000) paid this penalty.[20] On average, their total premiums (standard premium plus penalty) were about 32% higher than what they would have been had they not been subject to the penalty.

The penalty provision was included in the original Medicare legislation enacted in 1965 to help prevent adverse selection by creating a strong incentive for all eligible beneficiaries to enroll in Part B.[21] Adverse selection occurs when only those persons who think they need the benefits actually enroll in the program. When this happens, per capita costs are driven up, and premiums go up, thereby causing more persons (presumably the healthier, and less costly ones) to drop out of the program.[22] With most eligible persons over 65 enrolled in Part B, the costs are spread over the majority of this population and per capita costs are less than would be the case if adverse selection had occurred.

Those who receive premium assistance through a Medicare Savings Program do not pay this penalty; it is paid on their behalf by Medicaid. Additionally, for those disabled persons under 65 subject to a premium penalty, once the individual reaches age 65, he or she qualifies for a new enrollment period and would no longer pay a penalty.

Calculation of Penalty

The delayed enrollment penalty is equal to a 10% premium surcharge for each full 12 months of delay in enrollment and/or reenrollment during which the beneficiary was eligible for Medicare.[23] The length of the period equals: (1) the number of months that elapse between the end of the initial enrollment period and the end of the enrollment period in which the individual actually enrolls; or (2) for a person who re-enrolls, the months that elapse between the termination of coverage and the close of the enrollment period in which the individual enrolls.

Generally, individuals who do not enroll in Part B within a year of the end of their initial enrollment period would be subject to the premium penalty. For example, if an individual's initial enrollment period ended in September 2010 and the individual subsequently enrolled during the 2011 general enrollment period (January 1st through March 31st), the delay would be less than 12 months and the individual would not be subject to a penalty. However, if that individual delayed enrolling until the 2013 general enrollment period, the premium penalty would be 20%.

(Although the elapsed time covers a total of 30 months of delayed enrollment, the episode includes only two full 12-month periods.) An individual who waits more than 10 years to enroll in Part B would pay twice the standard premium amount.

The surcharge is calculated as a percentage of the monthly standard premium amount (e.g., in 2013, $104.90), and that amount is added to the beneficiary's premium each month.[24] For the example above, in which the individual is subject to a 20% premium penalty, the total premium in 2013 would be calculated as follows:

Premium Penalty = Standard Premium x Applicable Percentage
Standard premium + Premium Penalty = Penalty Adjusted Premium
Example of a 20% penalty in 2013: \$104.90 + (\$104.90 x 20%) = \$125.88

For those subject to the high-income premium (see "Income-Related Premium"), the late enrollment surcharge applies only to the standard monthly premium amount and not to the higher income adjustment portion of their premiums. Using the example above, should the beneficiary have an income of between \$85,000 and \$107,000, the applicable income-related adjustment of \$42.00 would be added onto the penalty adjusted premium of \$125.88, for a total monthly premium of \$167.88.[25]

There is no upper limit on the amount of the surcharge that may apply, and the penalty continues to apply for the entire time the individual is enrolled in Part B. Each year the surcharge is calculated using the standard premium amount for that particular year. Therefore, if premiums increase in a given year, the dollar value of the surcharge will increase as well.

Exemptions to Penalty

Under certain conditions, select beneficiaries may be exempt from the delayed enrollment penalty. Beneficiaries who are exempt include working individuals (and their spouses) with group coverage, some military retirees, some international volunteers, and those who based their non-enrollment decision on incorrect information provided by a federal representative. Individuals who are permitted to delay enrollment have their own *special enrollment periods* (SEP).

Current Workers

A working individual and/or the spouse of a working individual may be able to delay enrollment in Medicare Part B without being subject to the delayed enrollment penalty. Delayed enrollment is permitted when an individual 65 or over has group health insurance coverage based on the individual's or spouse's *current employment* (with an employer with 20 or more employees). About 1.7 million of the 2.8 million working aged population are enrolled in Part A only, with most of the rest enrolled in both Parts A and B.[26] Delayed enrollment is also permitted for certain disabled persons who have group health insurance coverage based on their own or a family member's *current employment* with a large group health plan. For the disabled, a large group health plan is defined as one which covers 100 or more employees.

Specifically, persons permitted to delay coverage without penalty are those persons whose Medicare benefits are determined under the Medicare secondary payer (MSP) program.[27] Under MSP, an employer (with 20 or more employees) is required to offer workers aged 65 and over (and workers' spouses aged 65 and over) the same group health insurance coverage that is made available to other employees. The worker has the option of accepting or rejecting the employer's coverage. If he or she accepts the coverage, the employer plan is primary (i.e., pays benefits first) for the worker and/or spouse over age 65, and Medicare becomes the secondary payer (i.e., fills in the gaps in the employer plan, up to the limits of Medicare's coverage). Similarly, a group health plan offered by an employer with 100 or more employees is the primary payer for its employees under 65 years of age, or their dependents, who are entitled to Medicare because of disability.[28]

Such individuals may sign up for Medicare Part B (or Part A) anytime that they (or their spouse) are still working, and they are covered by a group health plan through the employer or union based on that work. Additionally, those who qualify for Medicare based on age (i.e., over 65), may sign up during the 8-month period after employment or group health plan coverage ends, *whichever happens first.* Disabled individuals whose group plan is involuntarily terminated have six months to enroll without penalty.[29]

Individuals who fail to enroll during this special enrollment period are considered to have delayed enrollment and thus could become subject to the penalty. For example, even though an individual may have continued health coverage through the former employer after retirement or have COBRA coverage, he or she must sign up for Part B within 8 months of retiring to avoid paying a Part B penalty if the individual eventually enrolls. Individuals who return to work and receive health care coverage through that employment may be able to drop Part B coverage, qualify for a new special enrollment period upon leaving that employment, and re-enroll in Part B again without penalty as long as enrollment is completed within the specified timeframe.

Certain Military Retirees

Some military retirees may also be exempt from the late enrollment penalty. Health care coverage for military retirees was expanded by the Floyd D. Spence National Defense Authorization Act for FY2001 (P.L. 106-398). This law established the TRICARE For Life (TFL) program, which acts as a secondary payer to Medicare and provides supplemental coverage to

TRICARE-eligible beneficiaries who are entitled to Medicare Part A and have Medicare Part B, based on age, disability, or end-stage renal disease (ESRD). The Patient Protection and Affordable Care Act (ACA, P.L. 111-148, Section 3110) establishes a 12-month special enrollment period (SEP) for certain individuals who are otherwise eligible for TRICARE and are entitled to Medicare Part A based on disability or ESRD, but have declined Part B. The Secretary of Defense is required to identify and notify individuals of their eligibility for this Special Enrollment Period. The SEP begins the first day of the month following the end of the individual's initial enrollment period, or if later, the month the individual is notified that s/he is entitled to Medicare Part A and Part B. The late enrollment surcharge is waived for those who enroll during the SEP. (If the individual does not enroll during the SEP, he or she may only enroll during the General Enrollment Period and the late enrollment surcharge could apply.)

International Volunteers

Some international volunteers may also be exempt from the Part B late enrollment penalty. The Deficit Reduction Act of 2005 (P.L. 109-171) permits certain individuals to delay enrollment in Part B without a delayed enrollment penalty if they volunteered outside of the United States for at least 12 months through a program sponsored by a tax-exempt organization defined under Section 501(c)(3) of the Internal Revenue Code.[30] The individuals must demonstrate they had health insurance coverage while serving in the international program. Individuals permitted to delay enrollment have a six-month special enrollment period, which begins on the first day of the first month they no longer qualify under this provision.

Equitable Relief

Under certain circumstances, a special enrollment period may be created and/or late enrollment penalties may be waived if a Medicare beneficiary can establish that an error, misrepresentation, or inaction of a federal worker or an agent of the federal government (such as an employee of the Social Security Administration (SSA), CMS, or a Medicare administrative contractor) resulted in late Part B enrollment.[31] In order to qualify for an exception under these conditions, the beneficiary must provide documentary evidence of the error, which "can be in the form of statements from employees, agents, or persons in authority that the alleged misinformation, misadvice, misrepresentation, inaction, or erroneous action actually occurred."[32]

COLLECTION OF THE PART B PREMIUM

If a person is enrolled in both Medicare Part B and Social Security, the Part B premiums are deducted from the person's Social Security benefit.[33] In addition, railroad retirees and civil service annuitants have their Part B premiums deducted from their monthly checks when possible. This withholding does not apply to those beneficiaries receiving state public assistance through a Medicare Savings Program as their premiums are paid by their state Medicaid program (see "Premium Assistance for Low-Income Beneficiaries"). Beneficiaries who are not entitled to a monthly cash benefit from Social Security, a railroad retirement annuity or pension, or a federal civil service annuity must pay the Part B premium directly to CMS.[34]

Deduction of Part B Premiums from Social Security Checks

Ultimately, everyone who is eligible for Social Security retirement or disability benefits qualifies for Medicare. Most people who elect to participate in the Part B program pay the Medicare Part B premium.[35] By law, a Social Security beneficiary who is also enrolled in Medicare Part B must have the Part B premium automatically deducted from his or her Social Security benefits.[36] Automatic deduction from the Social Security benefit check also applies to Medicare Advantage participants, who are enrolled in private health-care plans in lieu of traditional Medicare.[37] About 65% of Social Security beneficiaries (37 million persons) have Medicare Part B premiums deducted from their benefit checks.[38] Social Security beneficiaries who do not pay Medicare Part B premiums include those who are under the age of 65 and don't yet qualify for Medicare (e.g., began receiving Social Security benefits at age 62), receive low-income assistance from Medicaid to pay the Part B premium, have started to receive Social Security disability insurance (SSDI) but are not eligible for Medicare Part B because they have not received SSDI for 24 months, or chose not to enroll in Medicare Part B. The amount of an individual's Social Security benefits cannot go down one year to the next as a result of the annual Part B premium increase, except in the case of higher-income individuals subject to income-related premiums. (See "Protection of Social Security Benefits from Increases in Medicare Part B Premiums.") For those beneficiaries "held-harmless," the dollar amount of their Part B premium increases would be held below or equal to the amount of the increase in their monthly Social Security benefits.

Part B Enrollees Who Do Not Receive Social Security Benefits

About 2% of Medicare Part B enrollees do not receive Social Security benefits. For example, certain persons who spent their careers in employment that was not covered by Social Security, including certain federal, state, or local government workers, and certain other categories of workers, do not receive Social Security benefits, but may still qualify for Medicare. For those who receive benefit payments from the Railroad Retirement Board (RRB),[39] or the Civil Service Civil Service Retirement System,[40] Part B premiums are deducted from the enrollees' monthly benefit payments but net retirement benefit amounts are not "held harmless" from increases in the Part B premium. For those who do not receive these types of benefit payments, Medicare will bill directly for their premiums every 3 months.[41] Nonpayment of premiums results in termination of enrollment in the Part B program, although a grace period (through the last day of the third month following the month of the due date) is allowed for beneficiaries who are billed and pay directly.[42]

Determining the Part B Premium

Each year, the CMS actuaries estimate total per capita Part B costs for beneficiaries aged 65 and older over for the following year and set the Part B premium to cover 25% of these expected expenditures.[43] However, because prospective estimates may differ from the actual spending for the year, contingency reserve adjustments are made to ensure sufficient income to accommodate potential variation in actual expenditures during the year. The Part B premium is a single national amount that does not vary with a beneficiary's age, health status or place of residence. Premiums may be adjusted, however, for late enrollment (see "Late-Enrollment Premium Penalty and Exceptions") and for beneficiaries with high incomes (see "Income-Related Premiums").

Premium Calculation for 2013[44]

Monthly Part B premiums are based on the estimated amount that would be needed to finance Part B expenditures on an incurred basis during the year. In estimating needed income and to account for potential variation, CMS takes into consideration the difference in prior years of estimated and actual program costs, the likelihood and potential impact of potential legislation affecting Part B in the coming year, and the expected relationship between incurred and cash expenditures (e.g., payments for some services provided during a particular year may not be paid until the following year). Once the premium has been set for a year, it will not be changed during that year.

While both aged and disabled Medicare beneficiaries may enroll in Part B, the statute provides that Part B premiums are to be based only on the expected benefit costs, i.e., the *monthly actuarial rate*, for the aged (those over 65). (See Appendix A for a discussion of the history of the premium methodology.) Part B costs not covered by premiums are paid for through transfers from the general fund of the Treasury. The monthly actuarial rates for *both* the aged and disabled enrollees are used to determine the needed amount of general revenue funding per beneficiary each month (one-half of the expected average monthly cost for each aged enrollee and one-half of the expected cost for each disabled enrollee).

To determine the 2013 monthly Part B premium amount, CMS first estimated the monthly actuarial rate for enrollees age 65 and older using actual per-enrollee costs by type of service from program data through 2011 and projected these costs for subsequent years. For 2013, CMS estimated that the monthly amount needed to cover one-half of the total benefit and administration costs for the aged would be $198.11. However, because of expected variations between projected and actual costs, a contingency adjustment of $14.07 was added to this amount (see “Contingency Reserve” below). After a reduction of $2.38 to account for expected interest on trust fund assets, the monthly actuarial rate for the aged was determined to be $209.80. As premiums are only based on projections of expected costs of the aged, and the actuarial monthly amount for the aged accounts for one-half of projections of total costs (with the actuarial monthly amount for the disabled making up the other half), the 2013 Part B premium amount is one-half of $209.80, or $104.90 per month (25% of the monthly expected per capita costs of the aged).

Contingency Reserve

The contingency reserve is the amount set aside to cover an appropriate degree of variation between actual and projected costs. In recent years, CMS has noted that Part B expenditures have been higher than expected under current law.[45] In some cases, legislation that resulted in increased Medicare

Part B expenditures for the year was enacted after the premium for the year had been set. For example, current law specifies a physician payment formula called the sustainable growth rate system (SGR) for calculating the annual update to the conversion factor used to determine payments under the physician fee schedule.[46] The SGR formula has called for a reduction in the update factor (i.e., lower reimbursement rates) for each year since 2003. However, Congress has overridden the payment cut in every year except one, by passing legislation that has either frozen or slightly increased the reimbursement rates. These actions have often led to discrepancies between the actual and projected Part B costs.

In calculating the premium for 2013, CMS recognized the possibility that Congress would override the scheduled reduction of about 27% in physician fees for 2013 (thereby significantly increasing Part B expenses), and provided for the maintenance of a somewhat higher contingency reserve than would otherwise be necessary in calculating the 2013 premium.[47]

Additionally, CMS assumed that the reduction in Medicare benefit payments under the Budget Control Act of 2011 (P.L. 112-25) scheduled to start in 2013 would be modified or postponed.[48] CMS estimated that Part B expenditures would be reduced by $4.3 billion in 2013 under sequestration. The contingency margin was adjusted to accommodate the possibility that sequestration would not occur.[49]

Additionally, starting in 2011, manufacturers and importers of brand-name drugs began paying a fee that is allocated to the SMI trust fund. The contingency reserve was thus reduced to account for this additional revenue. Further, certain payment incentives to encourage the development and use of health information technology (HIT) by Medicare physicians, are excluded from premium determinations. (HIT bonuses or penalties will be directly offset through transfers of general funds from the Treasury.) The downward 2013 contingency margin adjustment of $14.07 reflects the expected net effects of all of these factors.

INCOME-RELATED PREMIUMS

For the first forty-one years of the Medicare program, all Part B enrollees paid the same Part B premium regardless of their income. However, the Medicare Modernization Act of 2003 (MMA; P.L. 108-173)[50] required that, beginning in 2007, high-income enrollees pay higher premiums.[51] About 4% of Part B enrollees were estimated to have paid this higher premium in 2012.[52]

Adjustments are made to the Part B premiums for high-income beneficiaries with the share of expenditures paid by beneficiaries increasing with income. This share ranges from 35% to 80% of the value of Part B coverage. In 2013, individuals whose income exceeds $85,000, and couples whose income exceeds $170,000, are subject to higher premium amounts. Income thresholds used in determining high-income Part B premiums for 2011 through 2019 are frozen at the 2010 levels.[53] The current law provision that prevents a beneficiary's Social Security benefits from decreasing from one year to the next as a result of the Part B premium increase does not apply to those subject to an income-related increase in their Part B premiums. (See "Protection of Social Security Benefits from Increases in Medicare Part B Premiums.")

Determination of Income

To determine those subject to the high-income premium, Social Security uses the most recent Federal tax return provided by IRS. In general, the taxable year used in determining the premium is the second calendar year preceding the applicable year.

For example, the 2012 tax return (2011 income) was used to determine who would pay the 2013 high-income premiums.[54]

High-income adjustments to Part B premiums are referred to as the *income-related monthly adjustment amount* (IRMAA). The income definition on which these premiums are based is modified adjusted gross income (MAGI) which is different from total income. Specifically, gross income equals total income (from all sources) minus certain exclusions (e.g., nontaxable Social Security benefits). From gross income, adjusted gross income (AGI) is calculated to reflect a number of deductions, including trade and business deductions, losses from sale of property, and alimony payments. MAGI is defined as AGI[55] plus certain foreign earned income and tax-exempt interest.[56]

If a person had a one-time increase in taxable income in a particular year (such as from the sale of income producing property), that increase would be considered in determining the individual's total income for that year and thus liability for the income-related premium two years ahead. It would not be considered in the calculations for future years.

In the case of certain major life-changing events that result in a significant reduction in modified MAGI, an individual may request to have the determination made for a more recent year than the second preceding year.[57] Major life-changing events include (1) death of a spouse; (2) marriage; (3) divorce or annulment; (4) partial or full work stoppage for the individual or spouse; (5) loss by individual or spouse of income from income-producing property when the loss is not at the individual's direction (such as in the case of a natural disaster); or (6) reduction or loss for individual or spouse of pension income due to termination or reorganization of the plan or scheduled cessation of the pension.

If Medicare enrollees disagree with decisions regarding their income-related monthly adjustment amounts, they may file an appeal with Social Security.

Enrollees may either submit a "Request for Reconsideration"[58] or contact their local Social Security office to file an appeal. (An enrollee does not need to file an appeal if he or she is requesting a new decision based on a life-changing event described above, or if the enrollee has shown that Social Security used the wrong information to make the original decision.)

Income Thresholds and Premium Adjustments

Depending on their level of income, beneficiaries may be classified into one of five income categories.[59] In 2013, individuals with incomes less than $85,000 a year ($170,000 for a couple) pay the standard premium which is based on 25% of the average Part B per capita cost. Individuals with income over $85,000 per year and couples with income over $170,000 per year pay a higher percentage of Part B costs.

Depending on one's level of income over these threshold amounts, premiums may be adjusted to cover 35%, 50%, 65%, or 80% of the value of Part B coverage (with the rest being subsidized through federal general revenues).

The five income categories and associated premiums for 2013 are shown below in Table 2. When both members of a couple are enrolled in Part B, each pays the applicable premium amount.

Married persons who lived with their spouse at some point during the year, but who filed separate returns, are subject to different premium amounts. There are two higher income categories that determine the additional monthly premium adjustment for these beneficiaries. The income levels and premium amounts are shown in Table 3.

Table 2. Monthly Medicare Part B Premiums for 2013

Levels of Premium Adjustment and Percentage of Costs Covered by Premiums	Beneficiaries who file an individual tax return with income:	Beneficiaries who file a joint tax return with income:	Income-Related Monthly Adjustment Amount (IRMAA)	Total Monthly Premium (standard premium + adjustment)
Standard = 25%	Less than or equal to $85,000	Less than or equal to $170,000	$0.00	$104.90
Level 1 = 35%	Greater than $85,000 and less than or equal to $107,000	Greater than $170,000 and less than or equal to $214,000	$42.00	$146.90
Level 2 = 50%	Greater than $107,000 and less than or equal to $160,000	Greater than $214,000 and less than or equal to $320,000	$104.90	$209.80
Level 3 = 65%	Greater than $160,000 and less than or equal to $214,000	Greater than $320,000 and less than or equal to $428,000	$167.80	$272.70
Level 4 = 80%	Greater than $214,000	Greater than $428,000	$230.80	$335.70

Source: Centers for Medicare & Medicaid Services, "Medicare Program: Medicare Part B Monthly Actuarial Rates, Premium Rate, and Annual Deductible Beginning January 1, 2013," 77 *Federal Register* 69850, November 21, 2012, http://www.gpo.gov/fdsys/pkg/FR-2012-11-21/pdf/2012-28275.pdf.

Table 3. Part B Premium Adjustment for Married Beneficiaries Filing Separately for 2013

Beneficiaries who are married and lived with their spouse at any time during the year, but file a separate tax return from their spouse:	Income-Related Monthly Adjustment Amount (IRMAA)	Total Monthly Premium (standard premium +adjustment)
Less than or equal to $85,000	$0.00	$104.90
Greater than $85,000 and less than or equal to $129,000	$167.80	$272.70
Greater than $129,000	$230.80	$335.70

Source: "Medicare Program: Medicare Part B Monthly Actuarial Rates, Premium Rate, and Annual Deductible Beginning January 1, 2013," 77 *Federal Register* 69850, November 21, 2012, http://www.gpo.gov/fdsys/pkg/FR2012-11-21/pdf/2012-28275.pdf.

The original provision establishing the Part B income related premiums set the initial income threshold and high-income level ranges. Prior to 2010, annual adjustments to these levels were based on annual changes in the consumer price index for urban consumers (CPI-U), rounded to the nearest $1,000.

However, the ACA froze the income thresholds and ranges at the 2010 level through 2019, rather than allowing them to rise with inflation.[60] Therefore, the thresholds will remain at $85,000 and $170,000 through 2019. This means that over time, as income rises with inflation, including increases in Social Security benefits, a greater share of Medicare enrollees may pay the high-income premiums.

In 2020 and subsequent years, the income thresholds are again to be indexed to inflation as if they had not been frozen between 2011 and 2019.

Premium Assistance for Low-Income Beneficiaries

Medicare beneficiaries with limited income and resources may be able to qualify for assistance with their premiums and other out-of-pocket expenses.[61] About one in five Medicare beneficiaries receives Part B premium subsidies.

Medicare beneficiaries who qualify for full Medicaid benefits (full dual-eligibles) have the majority of their health care expenses paid for by either Medicare or Medicaid.

For these individuals, Medicaid covers the majority of Medicare premium and cost-sharing expenses, and supplements Medicare by providing coverage for services not covered under Medicare, such as dental services and long-term services and supports (LTSS).

In cases where services are covered by both Medicare and Medicaid, Medicare pays first and Medicaid picks up most of the remaining costs. Each state has different rules about eligibility and applying for Medicaid.[62]

Beneficiaries who do not meet their respective state's eligibility criteria for Medicaid may still qualify for assistance with Part B premiums if they have incomes of less than 135% of the federal poverty level (FPL) and assets of less than $7,080 for an individual or $10,620 for a couple in 2013.[63] These assistance programs are commonly referred to as *Medicare Savings Programs* (MSP).[64] Eligible individuals fall into one of the following coverage groups:

Qualified Medicare Beneficiaries (QMBs)

Aged or disabled persons with incomes at or below FPL may qualify for the QMB program.[65] In 2013, the QMB monthly qualifying income levels are $958 for individuals and $1,293 for a couple (annual income of $11,490 and $15,510, respectively).[66] QMBs are entitled to have their Medicare Parts A and B cost-sharing charges, including the Part B premium and all deductibles and coinsurance, paid for by Medicaid.[67] (See Table 4.) For QMBs, Medicaid coverage is limited to the payment of Medicare cost-sharing charges (i.e., the Medicare beneficiary is *not* entitled to coverage of Medicaid plan services, unless the individual is otherwise entitled to Medicaid).

Table 4. 2013 Medicare Savings Program Eligibility Standards

	Monthly Income[a]	Resources[b]	Benefits
Qualified Medicare Beneficiary (QMB)	At or below 100% FPL[c] $958 – single $1,293 – couple	$7,080 – single $10,620 – couple	Part B premium[d] Coverage of Parts A and B deductibles and coinsurance
Specified Low-Income Medicare Beneficiary (SLMB)	Above 100% but less than 120% FPL[c] $958.01 – $1,149 – single $1,293.01 – $1,551 – couple	$7,080 – single $10,620 – couple	Part B premium
Qualifying Individual (QI)	At or above 120% but less than 135% FPL[c] $1,149.01 – $1,293 – single $1,551.01 – $1,745 – couple	$7,080 – single $10,620 – couple	Part B premium

Source: Social Security Program Operations Manual Section HI 00815.023 (Income Limits), https://secure.ssa.gov/poms.nsf/lnx/0600815023, and CRS calculations based on the 2013 FPL Poverty Guidelines, http://aspe.hhs.gov/poverty /13poverty.cfm.

[a] These amounts do not include a $20 "disregard" where $20 from any income is not counted towards these income limits.

[b] Resources include money in checking and savings accounts, stocks, bonds, mutual funds, and Individual Retirement Accounts (IRAs). Resources don't include one's primary residence, a life insurance policy worth up to $1,500, one car, burial plots, up to $1,500 per person for burial expenses, and household items. Some states have no limits on resources.

[c] Federal Poverty Levels (FPLs) are updated each year, usually in January or February. Income levels are higher for Hawaii and Alaska and for those living with dependents.

[d] Most people do not pay a premium for Part A because they have worked 40 or more quarters in covered employment. For those without sufficient work history to qualify for premium-free Part A, Medicaid will also pay Part A premiums for QMBs.

Specified Low-Income Medicare Beneficiaries (SLMBs)

Individuals whose income is more than 100% but less than 120% of FPL may qualify for assistance as a SLMB. In 2013, the monthly income limits are $1,149 for an individual and $1,551 for a couple (annual income of $13,788 and $18,612, respectively).[68] Medicaid pays the Medicare Part B premiums for SLMBs, but not other cost-sharing.

Qualifying Individuals (QIs)

Individuals whose income is between 120% and 135% of the federal poverty level may qualify for assistance as QIs. In 2013, the monthly income limit for a QI is $1,293, and for a couple, $1,745 (annual income of $15,512 and $20,939, respectively). Medicaid protection for these individuals is limited to payment of the monthly Medicare Part B premium. Expenditures under the QI program are, however, paid for (100%) by the federal government from the Medicare SMI trust fund up to the state's allocation level.[69] A state is only required to cover the number of people who would bring its spending on these population groups in a year up to its allocation level. Any expenditures beyond that level are voluntary and paid entirely by the state. Funding for the QI program was first made available by the Balanced Budget Act of 1997 (BBA97; P.L. 105-33),[70] and was continued through subsequent legislation. Most recently, the American Taxpayer Relief Act of 2012 (P.L. 112-240) extended the program and the amounts available through allocation until December 31, 2013.[71]

Protection of Social Security Benefits from Increases in Medicare Part B Premiums

After a person becomes eligible to receive Social Security benefits, his or her monthly benefit amount is increased annually to maintain purchasing power over time. Near the end of each year, the Social Security Administration announces the cost-of-living adjustment (COLA) payable in January of the following year. The amount of the COLA is based on inflation as measured by the Consumer Price Index-Urban Wage Earners and Clerical Workers (CPI-W).[72] If the CPI-W decreases, Social Security benefits stay the same—benefits are not reduced during periods of deflation. In instances when the annual Social Security COLA is not sufficient to cover the standard Medicare Part B premium increase, most beneficiaries are protected by a *hold harmless* provision in the Social Security Act.[73] Specifically, if in a given year, the increase in the standard Part B premium would cause a beneficiary's Social Security check to be less, in dollar terms, than it was the year before, then the Part B premium is reduced to ensure that the amount of the individual's Social Security check does not decline.[74] To be held harmless in a given year, a Social Security beneficiary must have received Social Security benefit checks in both December of the previous year and January of the current year, and must also have had Part B premiums deducted from both checks.[75] The hold harmless provision operates by comparing the net dollar amounts of the two monthly benefit payments—if the net Social Security benefit for January of the current year is lower than in December of the previous year, then the hold harmless provision takes effect for most individuals.[76] This determination is made by the Social Security Administration.

Several groups are *not* covered by the hold harmless provision.

- **Lower-Income Beneficiaries.** Lower-income beneficiaries who receive premium subsidies are not held harmless for premium increases; however, the Medicaid program pays the full amount of any increase in their Part B premiums. (See "Premium Assistance for Low-Income Beneficiaries.")
- **Higher-Income Beneficiaries.** Higher-income beneficiaries who are required to pay income-related Part B premiums are not held harmless for premium increases. They are required to pay the full amount of any increase in their Part B premiums. (See "Income-Related Premiums.")
- **Beneficiaries with no history of Social Security benefit checks with deductions to cover the Medicare Part B premium.** This includes new enrollees in either Social Security or Medicare Part B, and Part B enrollees who do not receive Social Security benefits. As noted above, in order to be held harmless in a given year, a Social Security beneficiary must have received Social Security benefit payments in both December of the previous year and January of the current year, and must have had Part B premiums deducted from both checks. (See "Part B Enrollees Who Do Not Receive Social Security Benefits.")

As described earlier, an individual's Social Security COLA is determined by multiplying his or her benefit amount by the inflation rate (i.e., the CPI-W). Part B premiums are determined by projected Part B program costs. Thus, the number of people held harmless can vary widely from year to year, depending on annual inflation rates and projected Part B costs. For most years, the hold harmless provision has affected a relatively small number of beneficiaries. However, due to low inflation, no COLA adjustments were made to Social Security benefits in 2010 and 2011. Most Medicare beneficiaries (about 73%) were protected by the hold harmless provision and continued to pay the 2009 standard monthly premium of $96.40 in both 2010 and 2011.[77] Because Part B expenditures were still expected to increase in those years, and beneficiary premiums are required to cover 25% of those costs, the premiums for those not held harmless (27% of beneficiaries) were higher than they would have been had the rest of the beneficiaries not been held harmless. The standard monthly premiums paid by those not held harmless was $110.50 in 2010 and $115.40 in 2011.[78] In 2011, of the 27% who were not eligible to be held harmless, about 3% were new enrollees, about 5% were high-income, about 17% had their premiums paid for by Medicaid, and the remaining 2% did not have their premiums withheld from Social Security benefit payments.

In 2012, Social Security beneficiaries received a 3.6% COLA which increased the average monthly Social Security benefit payments by about $43 per month. This Part B premium increase was more than offset by the increase in Social Security benefits, and the hold-harmless provision was not applicable in 2012 for most beneficiaries. Similarly, the 2013 Social Security COLA of 1.7%[79] increased the average monthly Social Security benefit by about $21 per month,[80] which more than offset the $5 increase per month in standard Medicare premiums. Therefore, the hold-harmless provision will not be applicable to most beneficiaries in 2013.

PART B PREMIUMS OVER TIME

Part B premium changes through time generally reflect the growth in total Part B expenditures, although the exact relationship between Part B expenditures covered by the Part B premium has been changed by statute at various points. (See Appendix A.) The Part B premium has risen from $3.00 in 1966 to $104.90 in 2013. (See Figure 1.) For comparison, during a similar time period, average annual Part B benefit costs per beneficiary have increased from about $101 in 1970 (about $8.42 per month) to a projected $5,222 per beneficiary (about $435 per month) in 2012.[81]

Prior to 2000, the Part B premium decreased from year to year twice: once from 1989 ($31.90) to 1990 ($28.60) as a result of the repeal of the Medicare Catastrophic Coverage Act of 1988 (P.L. 100-360), and once from 1995 ($46.10) to 1996 ($42.50) as a result of the transition from a premium as determined by a fixed dollar amount under the Omnibus Reconciliation Act of 1990 (P.L. 101-508) to 25% of costs as directed under the Omnibus Budget Reconciliation Act of 1993 (P.L. 103-66).

More recently, because of the absence of a Social Security COLA in 2010 and 2011, most beneficiaries were "held-harmless" and paid the 2009 premium of $96.40 per month during those years. The standard 2010 and 2011 premiums, paid by those who were not held harmless, were thus higher than they would have been had the hold harmless provision not been in effect. (See "Protection of Social Security Benefits from Increases in Medicare Part B Premiums" for additional detail.)

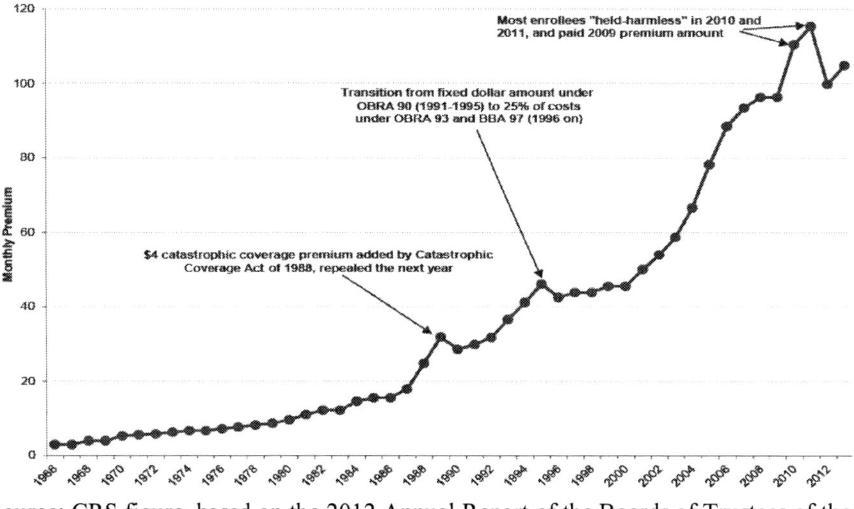

Source: CRS figure, based on the 2012 Annual Report of the Boards of Trustees of the Federal Hospital Insurance and Federal Supplemental Medical Insurance Trust Funds, Table V.E2 and Centers for Medicare & Medicaid Services, "Medicare Program: Medicare Part B Monthly Actuarial Rates, Premium Rate, and Annual Deductible Beginning January 1, 2013," 77 *Federal Register* 69850, November 21, 2012.

Figure 1. Monthly Medicare Part B Premiums; 1966-2013.

Since 2000, the Medicare Part B premium has more than doubled, increasing from $45.50 in 2000 to the current premium of $104.90 in 2013. Increases have been due to a number of factors that have increased per capita Part B expenditures during that time, including rising prices of health care services and equipment, new technologies, and increased utilization of Medicare Part B services. The CMS Office of the Actuary suggests that over the next 10 years, Part B premiums will increase more slowly than they have over the past decade, primarily due to ACA changes to Medicare payment methodologies that are expected to slow the rate of growth in spending for most Part B services.[82] Estimates of premiums in future years through 2021 may be found in Appendix C.

CURRENT ISSUES

Premium Amount and Annual Increases

The Medicare trustees estimate that over the next decade, Medicare Part B premiums will increase, on average, by over 5% each year. (See Appendix C.) Rising Medicare premiums could have a large effect on Social Security beneficiaries, particularly on those on those who rely on Social Security as their primary source of income. For example, among Americans aged 65 and older, 53% of married couples and 74% of unmarried persons receive more than half of their income from Social Security, and 23% of married couples and 46% of unmarried persons receive more than 90% of their income from Social Security.[83] Some of these beneficiaries may see a decline in their standard of living as their Medicare premiums rise.

Once a person has retired and elects to receive Social Security, his or her benefit is indexed to inflation and thereafter grows with annual Social Security COLAs.[84] However, Medicare premiums are based on the per capita cost growth of Part B benefits which reflect the growth in earnings of health care providers, and in the utilization and intensity of services used by beneficiaries, factors that have historically grown faster than CPI-U. This means that, over time, Medicare premiums represent a growing proportion of most beneficiaries' Social Security income.[85] Since 2000, Social Security's annual COLA resulted in a cumulative benefit increase of about 36%, significantly less than the Part B premium growth of close to 120%. The Medicare trustees estimated that average Part B plus Part D premiums in 2012 would represent close to 11% of the average Social Security benefit, and increase to an estimated 20% in 2086.[86]

Proposals to Modify the Late Enrollment Penalty

Periodically, proposals have been offered to modify or eliminate the Part B premium penalty either for all enrollees or alternatively for a selected population group. Some have suggested modifying the penalty provision to limit both the amount and the duration of the surcharge, such as is the case for delayed Part A enrollment which has a maximum 10% surcharge, and a duration of twice the number of years that enrollment was delayed. (See Appendix D for information on the Part A premium and late enrollment penalty.) Some have also suggested that Medicare Part B have a creditable coverage exemption, similar to that under Part D, that would allow Medicare beneficiaries with equivalent coverage to postpone enrollment in Part B without being subject be subject to a penalty. For example, under the Part D prescription drug benefit, individuals are not subject to a late enrollment penalty if they have maintained "creditable" prescription drug coverage prior to enrollment, i.e., coverage that is expected to pay at least as much as Medicare's standard prescription drug coverage.[87] Creditable prescription drug coverage includes such things as employer-based prescription drug coverage; qualified State Pharmaceutical Assistance Programs (SPAPs); and military-related coverage (e.g., VA and TRICARE).[88]

In recent Congresses, several bills have been introduced to address the Part B late enrollment penalty. For example, H.R. 1654, introduced in the 112th Congress, would have established a special Medicare Part B enrollment period for individuals enrolled in COBRA (Consolidated Omnibus Budget Reconciliation Act) continuation coverage who elected not to enroll in Part B during their initial enrollment period. The legislation would have also created a continuous enrollment period that would have allowed Medicare eligible beneficiaries to sign up for Part B outside of the general enrollment period, and receive health coverage the following month. Additionally, the proposed legislation would have directed the Government Accountability Office to study problems with Part B enrollment. Also introduced in the 112th Congress, H.R. 103 would have, among other changes, eliminated late-enrollment penalties for those between the ages of 65 and 70. In the 111th Congress, H.R. 2235 would have limited the penalty for late Part B enrollment to 10% and twice the period of no enrollment, similar to the Part A late enrollment penalty. It would also have excluded periods of COBRA and retiree coverage from the penalty.

Proposals to Require a Part B Premium Surcharge for Beneficiaries in Medigap Plans with Near First-Dollar Coverage

In addition to the payment of Part B premiums, Medicare beneficiaries enrolled in Parts A and B (traditional Medicare) must also pay other out-of-pocket costs when they use services, such as deductibles, co-payments, and co-insurance. Because this cost-sharing can be substantial, and there is no "catastrophic" cap on out-of-pocket spending, most Medicare beneficiaries have some form of supplemental coverage, for example, through Medicaid or an employer. About 30% of beneficiaries enrolled in traditional Medicare buy Medigap policies from private insurance companies which cover some or all of Medicare's cost-sharing. Individuals who purchase Medigap must pay a monthly premium which is set by, and paid to, the insurance company selling the policy.[89] There are 10 standardized Medigap plans with varying levels of coverage. Two of the 10 standardized plans cover Parts A and B deductibles and coinsurance in full (i.e., offer "first-dollar" coverage). In 2010, over 60% of all beneficiaries who purchased Medigap insurance were covered by one of these two plans. There is some concern that beneficiaries enrolled in Medigap plans with low-cost sharing requirements may have less incentive to consider the cost of health care services, and may thus increase costs to the Medicare program. Some have proposed imposing a Part B premium surcharge for Medicare beneficiaries who purchase certain types of Medigap plans. For example, the President's FY2013 budget proposal[90] would have imposed a Part B premium surcharge of approximately 15% of the average Medigap premium (about 30% of the Part B premium) for new Medicare beneficiaries who enroll in a near first-dollar Medigap plan.

Deficit Reduction

As Medicare currently represents about 13% of federal spending, most proposals to reduce federal deficits include suggestions to reduce Medicare program spending and/or increase program income. For example, some recent proposals would increase Medicare premiums as a portion of total program funding (i.e., decrease the amount of government subsidies). Certain proposals would limit premium increases to high-income beneficiaries. For example, the President's FY2013 budget proposal would have increased the applicable percentage of the program's cost per aged enrollee for higher income beneficiaries from the current 35% to 80% to between 40% and 90%. The proposal would have also continued the ACA freeze on income thresholds until 25% of beneficiaries were subject to the high-income premiums.

Other proposals would increase premiums paid by all beneficiaries. For example, a proposal introduced by Senators Lieberman and Coburn[91] suggests raising the standard Part B premium from the current 25% of program costs to 35% over five years. Finally, other proposals, such as that put forth in the FY2014 House Budget,[92] would place limits on the amount of the federal subsidy, and premiums would vary depending on the plan in which the beneficiary enrolled. In general, such "premium support" proposals would limit federal spending by changing the current Medicare program from a defined benefit to a defined contribution system.[93] Most such proposals limit the growth in the annual federal premium subsidy; for example, the House Budget proposal suggests a growth limit of GDP plus 0.5%. Depending on how such a proposal is designed, and should Medicare costs grow more quickly than the limit, beneficiary premiums could increase more rapidly than the amount of the premium subsidy. Some of the issues that would need to be addressed when evaluating these types of proposals include (1) the ability of Medicare beneficiaries to absorb increased costs given their current levels of income and assets, as well as their other out-of-pocket expenditures (both health and non-health related); (2) the willingness of high-income beneficiaries to continue participating in Medicare Part B should their premiums continue to increase; and (3) the capacity of the Medicaid program to continue providing premium assistance to low-income beneficiaries should premiums increase.

APPENDIX A. HISTORY OF THE PART B PREMIUM STATUTORY POLICY AND LEGISLATIVE AUTHORITY

The basis for determining the Part B premium amount has changed several times since the inception of the Medicare program, reflecting different legislative views of what share beneficiaries should bear as expenditures increased. When the Medicare program first went into effect in July 1966, the Part B monthly premium was set at a level to cover 50% of Part B program costs. Legislation enacted in 1972 limited the annual percentage increase in the premium to the same percentage by which Social Security benefits were adjusted for changes in the costof-living (i.e., COLAs). Under this formula, revenues from premiums soon dropped from 50% to below 25% of program costs because Part B program costs increased much faster than inflation as measured by the Consumer Price Index on which the Social Security COLA is based (Table A-1). From the early 1980s, Congress regularly voted to set Part B premiums at a level to cover 25% of program costs, in effect overriding the COLA limitation. The 25% provisions first became effective January 1, 1984, with general revenues covering the remaining 75% of Part B program costs. Premiums increased in 1989 as a result of the Medicare Catastrophic Coverage Act of 1988 (P.L. 100-360), which added a catastrophic coverage premium to the Part B premium. The Act was repealed in November 1989, and the Part B premium for 1990 fell as a result. Congress returned to the general approach of having premiums cover 25% of program costs in the Omnibus Budget Reconciliation Act of 1990 (OBRA 90, P.L. 101-508). However, OBRA 90 set specific dollar figures, rather than a percentage, in law for Part B premiums for the years 1991- 1995. These dollar figures reflected CBO estimates of what 25% of program costs would be over the five-year period. However, program costs grew more slowly than anticipated, in part due to subsequent legislative changes and as a result, the 1995 premium of $46.10 actually represented 31.5% of Medicare Part B program costs. The Omnibus Budget Reconciliation Act of 1993 (OBRA 93, P.L. 103-66) extended the policy of setting the Part B premium at a level to cover 25% of program costs for the years 1996-1998. As was the case prior to 1991, a percentage rather than a fixed dollar figure was used, which meant that the 1996 premium ($42.50) and the 1997 premium ($43.80) were lower than the 1995 premium ($46.10). BBA 97 permanently set the premium at 25% of program costs so that, generally speaking, premiums rise or fall with Part B program costs.[94]

The Medicare Prescription Drug, Improvement, and Modernization Act of 2003 (MMA, P.L. 108- 173), as modified by the Deficit Reduction Act of 2005 (DRA, P.L. 109-171), required that beginning in 2007, higher-income beneficiaries pay higher Part B premiums.[95] The income thresholds used to determine eligibility for the high-income premium are to be adjusted each year by the growth in the consumer price index.[96] The Patient Protection and Affordable Care Act (P.L. 111-148, Section 3402), however, froze these thresholds for the period of 2011 through 2019 at the 2010 levels.

Table A-1. Monthly Part B Premiums, 1966-2013

Year	Monthly premium	Effective date	Governing policy; legislative authority
1966	$3.00	7/66	Fixed dollar amount; Social Security Amendments (SSA) of 1965
1967	$3.00		Fixed dollar amount; SSA of 1965
1968	$4.00	4/68	Fixed dollar amount through March; Medicare Enrollment Act of 1967. Beginning April: 50% of costs; SSA of 1965
1969	$4.00		50% of costs; SSA of 1967
1970	$5.30	7/70	50% of costs; SSA of 1967
1971	$5.60	7/71	50% of costs; SSA of 1967
1972	$5.80	7/72	50% of costs; SSA of 1967
1973	$6.30	9/73	50% of costs; SSA of 1967 (COLA limit, added by SSA of 1972, could have applied, but was not needed). Limitations imposed by Economic Stabilization program set 7/73 amount at $5.80 and 8/73 amount at $6.10.
1974	$6.70	7/74	50% of costs; SSA of 1967 (COLA limit, added by SSA of 1972, could have applied, but was not needed)
1975	$6.70		Technical error in law prevented updating
1976	$7.20	7/76	COLA limit; SSA of 1972
1977	$7.70	7/77	COLA limit; SSA of 1972
1978	$8.20	7/78	COLA limit; SSA of 1972
1979	$8.70	7/79	COLA limit; SSA of 1972
1980	$9.60	7/80	COLA limit; SSA of 1972
1981	$11.00	7/81	COLA limit; SSA of 1972
1982	$12.20	7/82	COLA limit; SSA of 1972
1983	$12.20		Tax Equity and Fiscal Responsibility Act of 1982 (TEFRA) had set 25% rule for updates in 7/83 and 7/84. However, SSA of 1983 froze premiums 7/83-12/83 and changed future updates to January.
1984	$14.60	1/84	25% of costs; TEFRA, as amended by SSA of 1983
1985	$15.50	1/85	25% of costs; TEFRA, as amended by SSA of 1983

Table A-1. (Continued)

Year	Monthly premium	Effective date	Governing policy; legislative authority
1986	$15.50	1/86	25% of costs; Deficit Reduction Act (DEFRA) of 1984
1987	$17.90	1/87	25% of costs; DEFRA of 1984
1988	$24.80	1/88	25% of costs, Consolidated Omnibus Budget Reconciliation Act of 1985
1989	$31.90	1/89	25% of costs, OBRA 87, plus $4 catastrophic coverage premium added by Medicare Catastrophic Coverage Act of 1988
1990	$28.60	1/90	25% of costs; OBRA 89. Medicare Catastrophic Coverage Repeal Act of 1989 repealed additional catastrophic coverage premium, effective 1/90
1991	$29.90	1/91	Fixed dollar amount; OBRA 90
1992	$31.80	1/92	Fixed dollar amount; OBRA 90
1993	$36.60	1/93	Fixed dollar amount; OBRA 90
1994	$41.10	1/94	Fixed dollar amount; OBRA 90
1995	$46.10	1/95	Fixed dollar amount; OBRA 90
1996	$42.50	1/96	25% of costs; OBRA 93
1997	$43.80	1/97	25% of costs; OBRA 93
1998	$43.80	1/98	25% of costs; OBRA 93 and BBA 97
1999	$45.50	1/99	25% of costs; BBA 97
2000	$45.50	1/00	25% of costs; BBA 97
2001	$50.00	1/01	25% of costs; BBA 97
2002	$54.00	1/02	25% of costs; BBA 97
2003	$58.70	1/03	25% of costs; BBA 97
2004	$66.60	1/04	25% of costs; BBA 97
2005	$78.20	1/05	25% of costs; BBA 97
2006	$88.50	1/06	25% of costs; BBA 97
2007	$93.50	1/07	25% of costs; BBA 97 (MMA and DRA authorize higher premiums for high-income enrollees: 1st year of 3-year phase-in)

Year	Monthly premium	Effective date	Governing policy; legislative authority
2008	$96.40	1/08	25% of costs; BBA 97 (MMA and DRA authorize higher premiums for high-income enrollees: 2nd year of 3-year phase-in)
2009	$96.40	1/09	25% of costs; BBA 97 (MMA and DRA authorize higher premiums for high-income enrollees: 3rd year of 3-year phase-in)
2010	$110.50	1/10	25% of costs; BBA 97 (MMA and DRA authorize higher premiums for high-income enrollees, fully phased-in; hold-harmless provision applied to most enrollees who paid the 2009 rate of $96.40
2011	$115.40	1/11	25% of costs; BBA 97 (MMA and DRA authorize higher premiums for high-income enrollees, fully phased-in; ACA freezes income thresholds at 2010 levels from 2011 through 2019); hold-harmless provision applied to most enrollees who paid the 2009 rate of $96.40
2012	$99.90	1/12	25% of costs; BBA 97 (MMA and DRA authorize higher premiums for high-income enrollees, fully phased-in; ACA freezes income thresholds at 2010 levels from 2011 through 2019)
2013	$104.90	1/13	25% of costs; BBA 97 (MMA and DRA authorize higher premiums for high-income enrollees, fully phased-in; ACA freezes income thresholds at 2010 levels from 2011 through 2019)

Source: Various Annual Trustee Reports, including the 2012 Annual Report of the Board of Trustees of the Federal Hospital Insurance and Federal Supplementary Medical Insurance Trust Fund, April 2012; and Centers for Medicare & Medicaid Services, "Medicare Program: Medicare Part B Monthly Actuarial Rates, Premium Rate, and Annual Deductible Beginning January 1, 2013," 77 *Federal Register* 69850, November 21, 2012.

Appendix B. Standard and High-Income Part B Premiums and Income Thresholds: 2007-2013

Table B-1. Income Levels for Determining Medicare Part B Premium Adjustment and Per Person Premium Amounts 2007-2013 (in nominal dollars)

	2007	2008	2009	2010	2011	2012	2013
Standard Premium	Less than or equal to $80,000 individual Less than or equal to $160,000 couple $93.50	Less than or equal to $82,000 individual Less than or equal to $164,000 couple $96.40	Less than or equal to $85,000 individual Less than or equal to $170,000 couple $96.40[a]	Less than or equal to $85,000 individual Less than or equal to $170,000 couple $110.50[b]	Less than or equal to $85,000 individual Less than or equal to $170,000 couple $115.40[b]	Less than or equal to $85,000 individual Less than or equal to $170,000 couple $99.90	Less than or equal to $85,000 individual Less than or equal to $170,000 couple $104.90
Level 1	$80,001-$100,000 individual $160,001-$200,000 couple $105.80	$82,001-$102,000 individual $164,001-$204,000 couple $122.20	$85,001-$107,000 individual $170,001-$214,000 couple $134.90	$85,001-$107,000 individual $170,001-$214,000 couple $154.70	$85,001-$107,000 individual $170,001-$214,000 couple $161.50	$85,001-$107,000 individual $170,001-$214,000 couple $139.90	$85,001-$107,000 individual $170,001-$214,000 couple $146.90
Level 2	$100,001-$150,000 individual $200,001-$300,000 couple $124.40	$102,001-$153,000 individual $204,001-$306,000 couple $160.90	$107,001-$160,000 individual $214,001-$320,000 couple $192.70	$107,001-$160,000 individual $214,001-$320,000 couple $221.00	$107,001-$160,000 individual $214,001-$320,000 couple $230.70	$107,001-$160,000 individual $214,001-$320,000 couple $199.80	$107,001-$160,000 individual $214,001-$320,000 couple $209.80

	2007	2008	2009	2010	2011	2012	2013
Level 3	$150,001- $200,000 individual $300,001- $400,000 couple $142.90	$153,001- $205,000 individual $306,001- $410,000 couple $199.70	$160,001- $213,000 individual $320,001- $426,000 couple $250.50	$160,001- $214,000 individual $320,001- $428,000 couple $287.30	$160,001- $214,000 individual $320,001- $428,000 couple $299.90	$160,001- $214,000 individual $320,001- $428,000 couple $259.70	$160,001- $214,000 individual $320,001- $428,000 couple $272.70
Level 4	$200,000+ individual $400,000+ couple $161.40	$205,000+ individual $410,000+ couple $238.40	$213,000+ individual $426,000+ couple $308.30	$214,000+ individual $428,000+ couple $353.60	$214,000+ individual $428,000+ couple $369.10	$214,000+ individual $428,000+ couple $319.70	$214,000+ individual $428,000+ couple $335.70

Source: Centers for Medicare & Medicaid Services, Annual Notices, "Medicare Program; Medicare Part B Monthly Actuarial Rates, Premium Rate, and Annual Deductible," 2007 through 2012, and "Medicare Program: Medicare Part B Monthly Actuarial Rates, Premium Rate, and Annual Deductible Beginning January 1, 2013," 77 *Federal Register* 69850, November 21, 2012.

Note: When both are enrolled in Part B, each person in a couple pays the same individual premium amount.

[a] The standard Part B premium in 2009 was the same as that in 2008; however, the lack of change was not due to the "hold harmless" provision. CMS determined that 2008 premiums and revenues were slightly higher than needed to cover costs in that year, and that 2009 financing would be adequate at the same premium level.

[b] Due to no Social Security COLA in 2010 and 2011, most Part B enrollees were "held-harmless" and paid the 2009 standard monthly premium of $96.40.

Table B-2. Income Levels for Determining Part B Premium Adjustment for Married Beneficiaries Filing Separately and Associated Premiums 2007-2013 (in nominal dollars)

Income Level	2007	2008	2009	2010	2011	2012	2013
Standard	Less than or equal to $80,000 $93.50	Less than or equal to $82,000 $96.40	Less than or equal to $85,000 $96.40	Less than or equal to $85,000 $110.50	Less than or equal to $85,000 $115.40	Less than or equal to $85,000 $99.90	Less than or equal to $85,000 $104.90
Lower adjustment category	Greater than $80,000 and less than or equal to $120,000 $142.90	Greater than $82,000 and less than or equal to $123,000 $199.70	Greater than $85,000 and less than or equal to $128,000 $250.50	Greater than $85,000 and less than or equal to $129,000 $287.30	Greater than $85,000 and less than or equal to $129,000 $299.90	Greater than $85,000 and less than or $129,000 $259.70	Greater than $85,000 and less than or equal to $129,000 $272.70
Higher adjustment category	Greater than $120,000 $161.40	Greater than $123,000 $238.40	Greater than $128,000 $308.30	Greater than $129,000 $353.60	Greater than $129,000 $369.10	Greater than $129,000 $319.70	Greater than $129,000 $335.70

Source: Centers for Medicare & Medicaid Services, Annual Notices, "Medicare Program; Medicare Part B Monthly Actuarial Rates, Premium Rate, and Annual Deductible," 2007 through 2012, and "Medicare Program: Medicare Part B Monthly Actuarial Rates, Premium Rate, and Annual Deductible Beginning January 1, 2013," 77 *Federal Register* 69850, November 21, 2012.

Appendix C. Estimated Future Part B Premiums

Table C-1. Projected Part B Premiums

		Percentage of Program Costs Represented by Premium			
	25% (Standard)	**35%**	**50%**	**65%**	**80%**
2014	112.10	156.90	224.20	291.50	358.70
2015	117.00	163.70	233.90	304.10	374.20
2016	122.00	170.80	244.00	317.20	390.40
2017	128.20	179.40	256.30	333.20	410.10
2018	135.50	189.60	270.90	352.20	433.40
2019	143.60	201.00	287.10	373.20	459.40
2020	151.90	212.60	303.70	394.80	485.90
2021	161.20	225.60	322.30	419.00	515.70

Source: 2012 Report of the Medicare Trustees, Tables V.E2 and V.E3.

Notes: These figures only represent estimates of future premiums. Actual premiums are determined each year in the fall prior to the actual year the premium will be in effect. Additionally, these projections do not take into account legislation enacted subsequent to the issuance of the Trustees' report in May 2012 nor reflect economic assumptions that may have been updated since that time. The premiums above include an above-average contingency margin for the likely legislative override of the scheduled reduction in physician payment rates.

Appendix D. Part A Premiums

The vast majority of persons turning age 65 are automatically entitled to Medicare Part A based on their own or their spouse's work in covered employment. However, individuals age 65 and over who are not otherwise eligible for Medicare Part A benefits and certain disabled individuals who have exhausted other entitlement may voluntarily purchase Part A coverage.[97] In most cases, persons who voluntarily purchase Part A must also purchase Part B. The periods during which one can enroll are the same as those for Part B (see "Medicare Part B Eligibility and Enrollment").

The monthly Part A premium is equal to the full average per capita value of the Part A benefit ($441 per month in 2013). Persons who have at least 30 quarters of covered employment (or married to someone who has such coverage) pay a premium that is 45% less than the full Part A premium ($243 per month in 2013). CMS estimates that in 2013, about 604,000 individuals will voluntarily enroll in Part A by paying the full premium and about 50,000 will pay the reduced premium.[98]

Similar to Part B, a penalty is imposed for persons who delay Part A enrollment beyond their initial enrollment period (which is the same seven-month period applicable for enrollment in Part B).[99] However, both the amount of the penalty and the duration of the penalty are different than under Part B. Persons who delay Part A enrollment for at least 12 months beyond their initial enrollment period are subject to a 10% premium surcharge.[100] The surcharge is 10% regardless of the length of the delay. Further the surcharge only applies for a period equal to twice the number of years (i.e., 12-month periods) during which an individual delays enrollment. Thus, an individual who delays enrollment for three years under Part A would be subject to a 10% penalty for six years, whereas a person who delays enrollment for the same three-year period under Part B would be subject to a permanent 30% penalty.[101]

End Notes

[1] Estimates from the 2012 Annual Report of the Boards of Trustees of the Federal Hospital Insurance and Federal Supplementary Medical Insurance Trust Funds, https://www.cms.gov/Research-Statistics-Data-and-Systems/StatisticsTrends-and-Reports/ReportsTrustFunds/downloads/tr2012.pdf.

[2] For additional information on the Medicare program, see CRS Report R40425, *Medicare Primer*, coordinated by Patricia A. Davis and Scott R. Talaga.

[3] See CRS Report R41436, *Medicare Financing*, by Patricia A. Davis.

[4] For additional information see archived CRS Report R41128, *Health-Related Revenue Provisions in the Patient Protection and Affordable Care Act (ACA)*, by Janemarie Mulvey.

[5] Beneficiary premiums cover approximately 12.6% of the costs of "traditional" Medicare (Parts A and B combined), 12% from Part B premiums, and 0.6% from voluntary Part A premiums. See Appendix D for information on Part A premiums.

[6] Centers for Medicare & Medicaid Services, "Medicare Program: Medicare Part B Monthly Actuarial Rates, Premium Rate, and Annual Deductible Beginning January 1, 2013," 77 *Federal Register* 69850-69859, November 21, 2012, http://www.gpo.gov/fdsys/pkg/FR-2012-11-21/pdf/2012-28275.pdf.

[7] Depending on their level of income, beneficiaries subject to the income-related monthly adjustment pay a total monthly premium of 35%, 50%, 65%, or 80% of expected per capita Part B costs for the aged. See "Income-Related Premium."

[8] The 2013 Part B premium rates were published on November 21, 2012, *77 Federal Register 69850*, http://www.gpo.gov/fdsys/pkg/FR-2012-11-21/pdf/2012-28275.pdf.

[9] For additional information on Part A premiums, see Appendix D.

[10] For additional information on enrolling in Medicare, see Medicare publication "Understanding Medicare Enrollment Periods" at http://www.medicare.gov/Publications /Pubs/pdf /11219. pdf.

[11] See "Welcome to Medicare" publication at http://www.medicare.gov/Publications/Pubs/pdf /11095.pdf. When first becoming eligible for Medicare, beneficiaries need to make a number of choices regarding the benefits they wish to sign up for and how they wish to receive them. For example, new enrollees need to decide whether they wish to remain in traditional Medicare (Parts A and B, the default option) or if they would like to receive their A and B benefits through a private Medicare Advantage Plan (Part C). Additionally, beneficiaries will need to decide whether they would like to sign up for an outpatient prescription drug plan (Part D). These options are described in the "Welcome to Medicare" package. For free personalized health insurance counseling, beneficiaries may contact their local State Health Insurance Assistance Programs (SHIPs); contact information may be found at http://www.medicare.gov/ contacts/ and https://www.shiptalk.org/About /SHI Profile SearchForm.aspx.

[12] Those who live in Puerto Rico are not enrolled in Medicare Part B automatically. They need to sign up for it during the initial enrollment period or possibly be subject to a penalty. H.R. 670, introduced in the 113th Congress, would extend this automatic enrollment to residents of Puerto Rico and create a special enrollment period and reduce late enrollment penalties for those who did not sign up for Part B when first eligible.

[13] Should a beneficiary decline Part B coverage, a new Medicare card will be issued that indicates that the beneficiary has Part A coverage only.

[14] Individuals with Amyotrophic Lateral Sclerosis (ALS) are not subject to the 24 month waiting period and Medicare coverage begins the first day of the month during which disability benefits start. Additionally, the Medicare coverage period for persons diagnosed with end-stage renal disease (ESRD) generally begins in the third month after the month when dialysis begins.

[15] In the past, individuals were generally eligible to receive both full Social Security retirement benefits and Medicare coverage starting at age 65. However, the age to receive full retirement benefits has changed for some people, depending on the year they were born. For example, some people won't be eligible for full Social Security benefits until age 67. See http://www.ssa.gov/pubs/10530.html.

[16] To apply, individuals can call or visit their local Social Security office or call Social Security at 1-800-772-1213. Some people may also apply online if they meet certain rules, at http://www.ssa.gov/medicareonly/. For RRB retirees, application information may be found at http://www.rrb.gov/forms/opa/rb20/rb20.asp.

[17] An eligibility and enrollment date calculator may be found on the Medicare.gov website at http://www.medicare.gov/ MedicareEligibility/home.asp?version=default&browser=IE%7C8%7CWindows+7&language=English.

[18] For additional information on eligibility for the disabled under 65, see CRS Report RS22195, *Social Security Disability Insurance (SSDI) and Medicare: The 24-Month Waiting Period for SSDI Beneficiaries Under Age 65*, by Scott Szymendera.

[19] The Part B general enrollment period is different from the Medicare Advantage and Part D annual enrollment period which runs from October 15 to December 7 each year, with coverage effective the following January.

[20] Figures provided to CRS by the Centers for Medicare & Medicaid Services, March 2012.

[21] Social Security Act §1839(b).

[22] Specifically, adverse selection occurs when beneficiaries, who generally have more information than insurers about their own health status and expected health care needs, make insurance purchasing decisions based on their expected use of the insurance benefit. Their decision to purchase insurance is based on a comparison of the value of the insurance coverage, given their expected use, and the cost of the insurance. Should only (or disproportionately) persons who are high health care users enroll in the program, per capita costs would increase, thereby making the health insurance purchase decision less attractive for healthier, and presumably less costly, beneficiaries who then, in turn, might drop out of the program. Subsequent iterations of this cycle would drive premium costs higher and higher for a smaller and smaller subset of ever sicker and costlier beneficiaries.

[23] Social Security Act §1839(b).

[24] A late premium calculator may be found on the Medicare.gov website at http://www.medicare.gov/ MedicareEligibility/home.asp?dest= NAV%7CHome%7CResources%7 CSurcharge CalcQuestions%7CResourcesOverview&version=default&browser=IE%7C8%7C Windows+7&language=English.

[25] For additional information, see SSA Programs Operation Manual Section HI 01101.031, "How IRMAA is Calculated and How IRMAA Affects the Total Medicare Premium," at https://secure.ssa.gov/apps10/poms.nsf/lnx/0601101031.

[26] *Medicare Working-Aged Beneficiary Counts, Through December 2012*, from CMS 100% Unloaded Enrollment Database.

[27] Social Security Act §1837(i) and 42 CFR §407.20. See Medicare Publication "Medicare and Other Health Benefits: Your Guide to Who Pays First," http://www.medicare.gov /publications/pubs/pdf/02179.pdf and CMS Medicare Secondary Payer & You web page at https://www.cms.gov/Medicare/Coordination-of-Benefits/ MedicareSecondPayerandYou/index.html?redirect=/MedicareSecondPayerandYou/.

[28] For Medicare-eligible beneficiaries employed by organizations with fewer than 20 employees (or fewer than 100 employees for the disabled), Medicare generally pays primary and the employer group health plan is secondary. In such cases, employers may offer coverage that wraps around the Medicare benefit, and beneficiaries would need to enroll in Medicare Part B when first eligible to avoid a gap in coverage. Individuals who are turning 65 and still working should check with their employers' benefit administrator to learn how their employer health coverage works with Medicare.

[29] The Balanced Budget Act of 1997 (BBA, P.L. 105-33) added this exception to the penalty. This exception is for disabled persons who: (a) at the time they first become eligible for Part B are enrolled in a group health plan (regardless of size) by virtue of their current or former employment, and (b) whose continuous enrollment under the plan is involuntarily terminated at a time when their enrollment in the plan is by virtue of their or their spouse's former (i.e., not current) employment. These individuals have a special six-month enrollment period beginning on the first day of the month in which the termination occurs.

[30] Social Security Act §1837(k) and 42 CFR §407.21.

[31] Social Security Act §1837(h) and 42 CFR §407.32.

[32] For additional information, see Social Security Program Operations Manual Section HI 00805.170 *Conditions for Providing Equitable Relief*, https://secure.ssa.gov/poms.nsf/lnx /0600805170 and Section HI 00805.175 *Evidence of Government Error or Delay*, https://secure.ssa.gov/poms.nsf/lnx/0600805175.

[33] Social Security Act §1840(a)(1).

[34] 42 C.F.R. §408.60.

[35] Some beneficiaries do not pay Medicare premiums because they receive low-income assistance.

[36] Social Security Act §1840(a)(1).

[37] Beneficiaries who receive their Parts A and B benefits through Medicare Advantage (MA, Part C), must still pay the monthly Part B premium, but may pay different amounts. For example, some MA plans may offer an additional benefit by reducing the amount one pays for the Part B premium. Alternatively, some MA plans may be more expensive than traditional Medicare, for example because they provide benefits beyond what is provided under traditional Medicare, and may charge an additional premium in addition to the Part B premium. SSA has in place a "safety net" to prevent the deduction of more than $300 of Part C and Part D plan premiums from a single Social Security check. For amounts over $300, the enrollee may be billed directly.

[38] Number of people as of January 2013. Figures provided to CRS by the Social Security Administration.

[39] Social Security Act §1840(b)(1).

[40] Generally, employees of the federal government hired before 1984 are covered by the Civil Service Retirement System (CSRS) and are not covered by Social Security. Most federal workers first hired into federal service on or after January 1984, participate in the Federal Employees' Retirement System (FERS) which includes Social Security coverage.

[41] Payment may be made by check, money order, or credit card; or one may schedule it to be automatically deducted from one's bank account. Premium billing form and information may be found at https://secure.ssa.gov/poms.nsf/lnx/ 0600825914.

[42] This grace period may be extended for up to an additional three months if the enrollee can establish that non-payment was due to circumstances beyond his or her control, such as being physically or mentally incapable of making premium payments or due to an administrative error.

[43] Part B premium announcements are generally made in the fall prior to the effective year. For example, the Part B premium rate was announced in November of 2012.

[44] "Medicare Program: Medicare Part B Monthly Actuarial Rates, Premium Rate, and Annual Deductible Beginning January 1, 2013," 77 *Federal Register* 69850, November 21, 2012,http://www.gpo.gov/fdsys/pkg/FR-2012-11-21/pdf/ 2012-28275.pdf.

[45] Centers for Medicare & Medicaid Services, "Medicare Program: Medicare Part B Monthly Actuarial Rates, Premium Rate, and Annual Deductible Beginning January 1, 2013," 77

Federal Register 69850, November 21, 2012, http://www.gpo.gov/fdsys/pkg/FR-2012-11-21/pdf/2012-28275.pdf.

[46] For additional information on the Medicare physician rate system, see CRS Report R40907, *Medicare Physician Payment Updates and the Sustainable Growth Rate (SGR) System*, by Jim Hahn and Janemarie Mulvey.

[47] The American Taxpayer Relief Act of 2012 (P.L. 112-240), signed into law on January 2, 2013, prevented the reduction in Medicare physician payment rates slated to begin on January 1, 2013, and instead froze payment rates at their current level though December 31, 2013.

[48] For a comprehensive discussion of the BCA, see CRS Report R41965, *The Budget Control Act of 2011*, by Bill Heniff Jr., Elizabeth Rybicki, and Shannon M. Mahan. For Medicare specific rules under BCA, see CRS Report R42050, *Budget "Sequestration" and Selected Program Exemptions and Special Rules*, coordinated by Karen Spar.

[49] The American Taxpayer Relief Act of 2012 (P.L. 112-240), signed into law on January 2, 2013, postponed the automatic reduction by two months. See CRS Report R42884, *The "Fiscal Cliff" and the American Taxpayer Relief Act of 2012*, coordinated by Mindy R. Levit. No additional action has been taken, and payment reductions are scheduled to go into effect in April 2013.

[50] The MMA would have phased in the increase over five years; however, the Deficit Reduction Act of 2005 (DRA, P.L. 109-171) shortened the phase-in period to three years.

[51] At the time of enactment of the MMA, the Congressional Budget Office (CBO) estimated that 1.2 million persons (3% of beneficiaries) would pay higher premiums in 2007; and 2.8 million persons (6% of beneficiaries) would pay higher premiums in 2013. CBO further estimated that the MMA provision would reduce federal outlays by $13.3 billion over the 2007-2013 period. CBO estimated that the DRA provision accelerating the phase-in would increase premium collections by $1.6 billion over the 2007-2010 period. The MMA estimate and the DRA estimate were each made by CBO at the time of enactment of each law. Both estimates were based on the CBO budget baseline in effect at the time. As is the case for all CBO estimates, the earlier estimates are incorporated into subsequent CBO baselines. Therefore the two savings estimates cannot be added together.

[52] Centers for Medicare & Medicaid Services, "Medicare Program: Medicare Part B Monthly Actuarial Rates, Premium Rate, and Annual Deductible Beginning January 1, 2013," 77 *Federal Register* 69850, November 21, 2012, http://www.gpo.gov/fdsys/pkg/FR-2012-11-21/pdf/2012-28275.pdf.

[53] Section 3402 of the Patient Protection and Affordable Care Act (P.L. 111-148).

[54] If an enrollee amended his or her tax return and it changed the income used to determine the high-income adjustments, the updated information should be provided to Social Security so that it may correct or remove the income-related monthly adjustment amounts.

[55] Internal Revenue Code, Section 62.

[56] The definition of MAGI for IRMAA in Medicare is different from the MAGI definition in certain ACA Medicaid provisions. See CRS Report R41997, *Definition of Income for Certain Medicaid Provisions and Premium Credits in ACA*, coordinated by Janemarie Mulvey.

[57] Social Security Form SSA-44, http://www.ssa.gov/online/ssa-44.pdf.

[58] Social Security Form SSA-561-U2, http://www.ssa.gov/online/ssa-561.pdf.

[59] Social Security Act §1839(i).

[60] Section 3402 of the ACA (P.L. 111-148). Because more beneficiaries are expected to pay this higher premium over time and therefore reduce the amount of general revenues needed to

fund Part B, CBO scored this provision as saving the federal government $25 billion over 10 years (FY2010-FY2019), http://www.cbo.gov/sites/default/files/cbofiles/ftpdocs/113xx /doc11379/amendreconprop.pdf.

[61] See Medicare.gov, "Help with Medical and Drug Costs" at http://www.medicare.gov /navigation/medicare-basics/ medical-and-drug-costs.aspx. Subsidies are also available for low-income beneficiaries enrolled in Part D, the outpatient prescription drug benefit. Those who are eligible for assistance with Part B premiums through their Medicaid programs are automatically eligible to receive the Part D low-income subsidy. Other low-income beneficiaries with incomes below 150% of the federal poverty level, and who meet the resource tests, may also be eligible for the drug subsidy.

[62] See CRS Report RL33202, *Medicaid: A Primer*, by Elicia J. Herz.

[63] Income and asset requirements may vary by state and change each year. These amounts do not include a burial fund allowance of $1,500 per person.

[64] For additional information about these programs and to learn whether a beneficiary might qualify for Medicare premium assistance, one should contact one's State Medical Assistance (Medicaid) office. (As the names of these programs may vary by state, one should specifically inquire about Medicare Savings Programs.) The contact information for state Medicaid offices may be obtained by calling 1-800-MEDICARE (1-800-633-4227) or by visiting the following Medicare website: http://www.medicare.gov/contacts.

[65] The federal poverty levels for 2013 are $11,490 per year for an individual and $15,510 for a couple. (These levels are slightly higher in Alaska and Hawaii.) See *The 2013 HHS Poverty Guidelines* at http://aspe.hhs.gov/poverty/ 13poverty.cfm.

[66] The qualifying levels are slightly higher than the monthly federal poverty level because, by law, $20 per month of unearned income is disregarded in the calculation. See SSA Program Operations Manual HI 00815.023 Medicare Savings Programs Income Limits at https://secure.ssa.gov/poms.nsf/lnx/0600815023.

[67] The QMB program does not provide assistance with drug costs. Low-income beneficiaries who qualify for a Medicare Savings Program are automatically enrolled in Medicare Part D; their premiums and most cost-sharing is paid for by the Part D low-income subsidy which is financed through Medicare. States pay some of the costs for Part D low- income assistance through state transfer payments.

[68] The qualifying levels are calculated the same way as for the QMB program.

[69] In general, Medicaid payments are normally shared between the federal government and the states according to matching formulas.

[70] Section 4732(c) of BBA97 added §1933(c) of the Social Security Act.

[71] See CRS Report R42944, *Medicare, Medicaid, and Other Health Provisions in the American Taxpayer Relief Act of 2012*, coordinated by Jim Hahn.

[72] The CPI-W tracks the prices of a fixed market basket of goods and services over time. Social Security's COLA is calculated as the change in the CPI-W from the third quarter of the prior calendar year to the third quarter of the current calendar year. If the CPI-W increases during this period, Social Security benefits for the next year increase proportionately. See CRS Report 94-803, *Social Security: Cost-of-Living Adjustments*, by Gary Sidor.

[73] Social Security Act §1839(f). The hold harmless provision was first implemented in January 1987.

[74] For more information on the hold harmless provision, see CRS Report R40561, *Interactions Between the Social Security COLA and Medicare Part B Premiums*, by Jim Hahn.

[75] Note that Social Security benefit checks reflect benefit entitlements for the previous month while Part B premiums are deducted in advance. For example, a November Social Security

benefit check is not received until December, but has December's Part B premium deducted from it.

[76] Part D premiums are not covered by the hold harmless provision; therefore some people protected by the Part B hold harmless provision may still see a decrease in their Social Security checks due to an increase in Medicare Part D premiums. Beneficiaries who qualify for the Part D low-income subsidies, however, would not be affected.

[77] The standard Part B premium in 2009 was also the same as that in 2008, $96.40; however, the lack of change in those years was not a result of the "hold harmless" provision. At the end of 2008, it was determined that Part B premiums and general revenue financing in recent years had been set at somewhat higher levels than would otherwise be required to maintain an adequate contingency reserve, and that the level of assets in the Part B account of the SMI trust fund were more than adequate. Therefore, it was estimated that an adequate level of assets could be maintained throughout the next year, 2009, without an increase in premiums.

[78] Most new enrollees in 2010 were eligible to be held harmless in the second year of no COLA, i.e., 2011; these individuals continued to pay the 2010 standard premium of $110.50 in 2011.

[79] Social Security Administration, "Cost-of-Living Adjustment (COLA) Information for 2013," http://www.socialsecurity.gov/cola/.

[80] SSA Fact Sheet, "2013 Social Security Changes," http://www.ssa.gov/pressoffice /factsheets/ colafacts2013.htm.

[81] For additional information on Part B and total Medicare cost growth, see CRS Report R41436, *Medicare Financing*, by Patricia A. Davis. For data on recent growth in specific Part B benefits, see the 2012 Report of the Medicare Trustees, pp. 146-161, https://www.cms.gov/ Research-Statistics-Data-and-Systems/Statistics-Trends-and-Reports/ ReportsTrustFunds/downloads/tr2012.pdf.

[82] The ACA did not make changes to the physician payment rate (SGR) formula. Solomon M. Mussey, CMS Office of the Actuary, Estimated Effects of the "Patient Protection and Affordable Care Act," as Amended, on the Year of Exhaustion for the Part A Trust Fund, Part B Premiums, and Part A and Part B Coinsurance Amounts, April 22, 2010, http://www.cms.gov/Research-Statistics-Data-and-Systems/Research/ActuarialStudies/ downloads/ PPACA_Medicare_2010-04-22.pdf.

[83] Social Security Basic Facts, http://www.ssa.gov/pressoffice/basicfact.htm.

[84] The COLA increases the benefits paid to *current* beneficiaries. In contrast, average Social Security benefits (those paid to new and current beneficiaries) have risen at a faster rate than the annual COLA, because the formula for calculating initial Social Security benefits is linked to *wage* growth, whereas the COLA is based on *price* growth. Generally, wages rise faster than prices.

[85] A "hold harmless" provision, described earlier, caps the annual Part B premium increase (but not the Part D increase) at the dollar amount of a beneficiary's COLA.

[86] Similarly, average cost-sharing was estimated to be about 13% of the Social Security benefit in 2012, and expected to increase to approximately 24% in 2086. *2012 Annual Report of the Boards of Trustees of the Federal Hospital Insurance and Federal Supplemental Medical Insurance Trust Funds*, pp. 41-42, https://www.cms.gov/ResearchStatistics-Data-and-Systems/Statistics-Trends-and-Reports/ReportsTrustFunds/downloads/tr2012.pdf.

[87] See Medicare publication "Your Guide to Medicare Prescription Drug Coverage," http://www.medicare.gov/ Publications/Pubs/pdf/11109.pdf, p. 17.

[88] Employers or unions may also qualify for a federal subsidy to maintain prescription drug coverage for their retirees. Such subsidies are generally less expensive to the federal government than providing full coverage to such enrollees under Part D. *2012 Annual Report of the Boards of Trustees of the Federal Hospital Insurance and Federal Supplemental Medical Insurance Trust Funds*, https://www.cms.gov/Research-Statistics-Data-and-Systems/StatisticsTrends-and-Reports/ReportsTrustFunds/downloads/tr2012.pdf, Tables II.B1 and IV.B10.

[89] See CRS Report R42745, *Medigap: A Primer*, by Carol Rapaport.

[90] See CRS Report R42368, *Centers for Medicare & Medicaid Services: President's FY2013 Budget*, coordinated by Alison Mitchell and Paulette C. Morgan.

[91] *A Bipartisan Plan to Save Medicare and Reduce Debt*, June 28, 2011, http://www.coburn.senate.gov/public//index.cfm?a=Files.Serve&File_id=1ea8e116-6d15-46ba-b2e0-7312585 83305.

[92] See CRS Report R43017, *Overview of Health Care Changes in the FY2014 Budget Proposal Offered by House Budget Committee Chairman Ryan*, by Patricia A. Davis, Alison Mitchell, and Bernadette Fernandez.

[93] Most premium support models combine Parts A and B benefits, and the premium subsidy and beneficiary premiums would apply to both of these parts of Medicare.

[94] BBA 97 made a change that had the effect of increasing the Part B premium over time. Prior to BBA 97, both Parts A and B of Medicare covered home health services. Payments were made under Part A, except for those few persons who had no Part A coverage. In order to extend the solvency of the Part A (hospital insurance) trust fund, BBA 97 gradually transferred coverage of some home health visits from Part A to Part B. Beginning January 1, 2003, Part A covers only post-institutional home health services for up to 100 visits, except for those persons with Part A coverage only who are covered without regard to the post-institutional limitation. Part B covers other home health services.

[95] MMA increased the Part B premium percentage for high-income enrollees; DRA accelerated the phase-in period for such premiums.

[96] Social Security Act §1839(i)(5).

[97] An individual eligible to enroll must be a resident of the United States. Further, the individual must either be a citizen or an alien lawfully admitted for permanent residence who has resided in the United States continuously for the immediately preceding five years. Section 1818A of the Social Security Act provides for voluntary enrollment in Medicare Part A for certain disabled individuals who were entitled to coverage due to their receipt of disability benefits, but who have lost those benefits because they have returned to work and their incomes exceed the level of "substantial gainful activity." For additional information on Part A benefits for the disabled returning to work, see Social Security website "Working While Disabled," http://www.socialsecurity.gov/pubs/10095.html.

[98] "Medicare Program; Medicare Part A Premiums for CY 2013 for the Uninsured Aged and for Certain Disabled Individuals Who Have Exhausted Other Entitlement," 77 *Federal Register* 69859, November 21, 2012, http://www.gpo.gov/fdsys/pkg/FR-2012-11-21/pdf/2012-28274.pdf.

[99] The Consolidated Appropriations Act of 2001 (P.L. 106-554) exempts certain state and local retirees, retiring prior to January 1, 2002, from the Part A delayed enrollment penalty. These are groups of persons for whom the state or local government elects to pay the Part A delayed enrollment penalty for life. The amount of the penalty which would otherwise be assessed is to be reduced by an amount equal to the total amount of Medicare payroll taxes

paid by the employee and the employer on behalf of the employee. The provision applies to premiums beginning January 2002.

[100] Similar to Part B, if one qualifies for and signs up during a special enrollment period, e.g., within 8 months of retiring, one may not be subject to a penalty.

[101] Prior to enactment of the Consolidated Omnibus Budget Reconciliation Act of 1985 (COBRA; P.L. 99-272), there was no upper limit on the amount of the Part A surcharge or duration of the surcharge. COBRA limited the amount of the Part A surcharge to 10% and the duration to twice the period of delayed enrollment.

In: Medicare Part B
Editor: Ricardo Visser

ISBN: 978-1-62808-097-1

Chapter 2

MEDICARE: HIGH-EXPENDITURE PART B DRUGS*

United States Government Accountability Office

Washington, DC 20548
October 12, 2012

The Honorable Herb Kohl
Chairman
Special Committee on Aging United States Senate

The Honorable Dick Durbin
United States Senate

In 2010, the Medicare program and its beneficiaries spent about $19.5 billion on Part B drugs[1]—drugs that are commonly administered by a physician or under a physician's close supervision in physicians' offices and hospital outpatient departments.[2] Some of these drugs are particularly expensive for Medicare, either because they are used by a large number of beneficiaries or because their prices are high. These drugs generally differ from drugs beneficiaries obtain through Medicare Part D, which are usually self-administered and for which Medicare, its beneficiaries, and the states spent $61.7 billion in 2010.[3]

* This is an edited, reformatted and augmented version of United States Government Accountability Office, Publication No. GAO-13-46R, dated October 12, 2012.

Medicare bases its payments for most Part B drugs on the average sales price (ASP), which is calculated from data that manufacturers report quarterly to the Centers for Medicare & Medicaid Services (CMS), the agency within the Department of Health and Human Services that administers Medicare. ASP is the average price, after rebates and discounts, of all sales of a specified drug in the United States; consequently, Medicare's payment rates for Part B drugs are based on prices set by the private market.

You asked us to analyze trends in utilization and expenditures for high-expenditure Part B drugs and to estimate Medicare's proportion of total U.S. expenditures for these high-expenditure drugs. This report examines (1) the Part B drugs for which Medicare expenditures were highest in 2010 and the utilization and spending trends for these high-expenditure Part B drugs from 2008 to 2010, and (2) nationwide spending levels for the total U.S. population for these high-expenditure Part B drugs in 2010 and Medicare's percentage of total U.S. spending.

To identify the highest-expenditure Part B drugs in 2010 (the latest year for which data were available) and examine their utilization and spending trends, we used the CMS National Claims History 5 Percent Sample for physician, hospital outpatient, and durable medical equipment (DME) claims for 2008, 2009, and 2010.[4] We calculated the total amount spent on each Part B-covered drug in 2010 by the Medicare fee-for-service (FFS) program and by or on behalf of its beneficiaries and then ranked the drugs by total expenditures.[5] We identified the 55 drugs with the highest total 2010 Medicare expenditures—that is, expenditures by the Medicare program and expenditures by or on behalf of beneficiaries—and examined the number of beneficiaries using each of these drugs and the average annual cost per beneficiary.[6] For these 55 drugs, we also examined changes in total expenditures, beneficiary utilization, and prices from 2008 to 2010. We obtained information on the purpose and other characteristics of these drugs from the Food and Drug Administration (FDA), the National Institutes of Health (NIH), and manufacturers.

To estimate Medicare's share of total U.S. spending for these 55 high-expenditure Part B drugs, we obtained estimates of total 2010 U.S. expenditures—excluding Medicare FFS—for each of the drugs from IMS Health, a company that collects and analyzes health care data. To make these estimates, IMS Health used its national claims database, which contains commercial health plan claims for more than 60 million unique patients from more than 80 health plans across the United States.[7] IMS Health used claims for all beneficiaries who had been enrolled throughout 2010, but removed claims from Medicare supplemental health insurance policies to avoid double counting these claims, which were also included in the Medicare claims. IMS Health then used age-gender population information reported by the U.S. Census to project its claims data to the entire insured U.S. population, excluding the Medicare FFS population. To estimate total spending and utilization for the U.S. non-Medicare population, IMS Health made the assumption that beneficiaries not included in IMS Health's claims database, including those insured through certain government programs such as Medicaid, the Veterans Health Administration, and TRICARE,[8] had expenditures similar to the commercially insured population of the same age and gender. We used these projections plus 2010 Medicare FFS claims to estimate the spending on each of the 55 drugs for the total U.S. insured population in 2010, thereby enabling us to estimate Medicare's share of spending for these drugs.

While we believe our analytical approach allows us to achieve our objectives, our analysis has some limitations. IMS Health projected expenditures from a large national claims database but, by definition, projections are subject to error. Furthermore, according to IMS Health, hospital outpatient expenditures are underrepresented by an unknown amount. To the extent that Part B drugs may, in certain circumstances, be paid under Part A, Medicare expenditures and utilization are also underrepresented by an unknown amount in the estimates of total U.S. expenditures.

We ensured the reliability of the Medicare claims data used in this report by performing appropriate electronic data checks and by interviewing agency officials who were knowledgeable about the data. We also checked total expenditures for the 55 highest-expenditure Part B drugs in the claims data against the published total expenditures for these drugs in CMS's Part B National Summary Files.[9]

IMS Health removed from its claims database cases where expenditure fields were not populated, and in cases where the paid amount was greater than the allowed amount, replaced the paid amount with the allowed amount. It also allowed only three claims per patient per day per code. When there were more than three, the three claims with the largest allowed amounts were retained. We found that the Medicare and IMS data were sufficiently reliable for the purposes of our analysis.

We conducted our work from August 2011 through August 2012 in accordance with all sections of GAO's Quality Assurance Framework that are relevant to our objectives. The framework requires that we plan and perform the engagement to obtain sufficient and appropriate evidence to meet our stated objectives and to discuss any limitations to our work. We believe that the information and data obtained, and the analysis conducted, provide a reasonable basis for any findings and conclusions.

RESULTS IN BRIEF

In 2010, the 55 highest-expenditure Part B drugs represented $16.9 billion in spending, or about 85 percent of all Medicare spending on Part B drugs, which totaled $19.5 billion.

The number of Medicare beneficiaries who received each of these drugs varied from 15.2 million receiving the influenza vaccines to 660 hemophilia A patients receiving a group of biologicals known collectively as factor viii recombinant, which had the largest average annual cost per beneficiary—$217,000.[10] Our analysis showed that most of the 55 drugs increased in expenditures, prices, and average annual cost per beneficiary from 2008 to 2010.

The 5 drugs with the largest increase in Medicare expenditures over this time period also had the largest increase in the number of beneficiaries receiving each drug. Four of the 10 drugs which showed the greatest increase in expenditures were also among the 10 drugs showing the greatest price increases.

Spending on Medicare beneficiaries accounted for the majority of estimated total U.S. spending for 35 of the 55 highest-expenditure Part B drugs in 2010. For 17 of the 35, Medicare spending accounted for more than two-thirds of total U.S. spending, defined as spending by the insured population in the United States.

BACKGROUND

Medicare Part B generally covers drugs and biologicals administered under a physician's direct supervision, including those administered in physician offices and in hospital outpatient departments that are not usually self-administered. These include drugs infused through DME, certain vaccines (influenza, pneumococcal, and hepatitis B)[11], osteoporosis drugs, oral cancer drugs if the same drug is available in injectable form, antinausea drugs used as part of an anticancer chemotherapeutic regimen, erythropoiesis-stimulating agents,[12] blood clotting factors for hemophilia patients, injectable drugs, and immunosuppressive drugs for transplant patients. The Medicare program pays 80 percent of the expenditures for Part B drugs and the beneficiary is responsible for the remaining 20 percent, which may be paid by supplemental coverage such as a Medicare supplemental health insurance policy,[13] an employer-sponsored retiree health plan, or Medicaid. As of 2009, nearly 90 percent of Medicare Part B beneficiaries had some form of supplemental coverage.

Payment to physicians is set at 106 percent of ASP for most Part B drugs they administer; however, payment for some Part B drugs is set on a different basis. Vaccines, infusion drugs furnished through DME, and blood products are paid at 95 percent of average wholesale price (AWP), which is the manufacturer's average price to wholesalers.[14]

In cases where the ASP of a new drug during the first quarter of sales is unavailable, payment may be set at 106 percent of the wholesale acquisition cost (WAC), which is the manufacturer's list price to wholesalers. If the WAC is not yet available for the new drug, payment is based on the invoice price. Payment for Part B drugs administered in hospital outpatient departments is determined based on ASP, though the rate can vary from year to year. In 2010, it was 104 percent of ASP.[15]

Additionally, for certain drugs such as drugs used to treat cancer, some new drugs, and orphan drugs,[16] which are drugs used to treat rare diseases, Medicare makes additional payments for some drugs administered in the hospital outpatient setting, known as transitional pass-through payments, which can be paid for 2 to 3 years.[17] For new drugs, pass-through status is intended to make the drugs accessible to beneficiaries while a pricing history is developed and the price is established.

New drugs can be patented and, while under patent, can be manufactured or sold solely by the patent holder. Patents generally last for 20 years from the date of application.[18] After the patent expires and generic forms of the drug are marketed at significantly lower prices, the price of the original drug usually falls.[19]

Orphan drug status is granted by FDA to drugs that treat rare diseases—those that affect fewer than 200,000 people in the United States or for which there is no reasonable expectation of recovering the costs of development and marketing—and confers several benefits on the drug sponsor, including a 7-year period of market exclusivity.[20]

The Highest-Expenditure Medicare Part B Drugs Represented Most Part B Drug Spending in 2010 and Most Showed Increases in Spending, Utilization, and Price from 2008 to 2010

The 55 highest-expenditure Part B drugs accounted for 85 percent of all Part B drug spending in 2010. Utilization and annual spending per beneficiary for these drugs varied widely, but, like spending, generally increased between 2008 and 2010. Enclosure I contains a complete list of the 55 highest-expenditure Part B drugs in 2010.

Fifty-five Highest-Expenditure Part B Drugs Accounted for Three-Quarters of Part B Drug Expenditures in 2010

In 2010, the 55 highest-expenditure Part B drugs represented $16.9 billion in spending, or about 85 percent of all Medicare spending on Part B drugs, which totaled $19.5 billion. The 10 highest-expenditure Part B drugs accounted for about 45 percent of all Part B drug spending in 2010. Eight of the 10 most expensive were biological products as shown in table 1, and 4 of the 10 had orphan drug marketing exclusivity in 2010.[21] None of the 10 highest-expenditure drugs had a generic version approved by FDA in 2010. Enclosure II provides information on the expenditures, utilization, and average annual per beneficiary cost for the 55 Part B drugs. Enclosure III provides a list of all the 55 drugs that had orphan drug marketing exclusivity in 2010. Enclosure IV provides information on the generic availability of the 55 highest-expenditure Part B drugs.

Medicare spent most—$2 billion—on the drug Epogen/Procrit[22] for the treatment of anemia in end-stage renal disease (ESRD) patients.[23] The second most expensive drug was Rituxan, which is used to treat non-Hodgkin's lymphoma, a type of cancer, and rheumatoid arthritis. Lucentis, the third most expensive drug, is used to treat wet age-related macular degeneration (AMD), an eye condition, and during this period Avastin, a cancer drug which was the fourth most expensive, also was used off-label to treat wet AMD.[24] There was considerable interest by physicians and other experts in using Avastin for this purpose in part because the expenditure per treatment was significantly less than for Lucentis. However, it was not known whether Avastin was comparable to Lucentis in efficacy. A clinical trial determined that Avastin and Lucentis were equally effective, but the first trial results were not available until 2011, and so did not affect utilization in 2010.

Table 1. Ten Highest-Expenditure Medicare Part B Drugs, 2010

2010 rank by total Medicare expenditures	Brand name(s)	Drug description	Classification	Condition(s) treated	Total 2010 expenditures for Medicare beneficiaries (dollars in millions)
1	Epogen/Procrit (ESRD use)	Epoetin alfa, ESRD[a]	Biological	Anemia in end-stage renal disease (ESRD) patients	$2,000
2	Rituxan [b]	Rituximab injection	Biological	Cancer; rheumatoid arthritis	1,302
3	Lucentis	Ranibizumab injection	Biological	Wet age-related macular degeneration (AMD)	1,180
4	Avastin [b]	Bevacizumab injection	Biological	Cancer; wet AMD	1,130
5	Remicade [b]	Infliximab injection	Biological	Various autoimmune disorders	900
6	Neulasta	Injection, pegfilgrastim 6mg	Biological	Prevent infection in chemotherapy patients	888
7	Aranesp (non-ESRD use)	Darbepoetin alfa, non-ESRD	Biological	Anemia in chemotherapy patients	504
8	Epogen/Procrit (non-ESRD use)	Epoetin alfa, non-ESRD	Biological	Anemia in chemotherapy and HIV patients; prevent blood loss in surgical patients	443
9	Alimta[b]	Pemetrexed injection	Drug	Cancer	394
10	Taxotere	Docetaxel injection	Drug	Cancer	387
	Total				$9,128

Source: GAO analysis of CMS, FDA, NIH, and drug manufacturer data.

[a] End-stage renal disease (ESRD) is also known as stage 5 chronic kidney disease.

[b] These products had orphan drug marketing exclusivity for specific FDA-approved indications in 2010.

Of the 55 highest-expenditure Part B drugs, cancer and its side effects were treated by more drugs (23 drugs) than any other set of conditions in 2010. (See figure 1.) Other conditions that were treated by several drugs included immune system disorders such as rheumatoid arthritis (13 drugs) and chronic kidney disease (5 drugs).

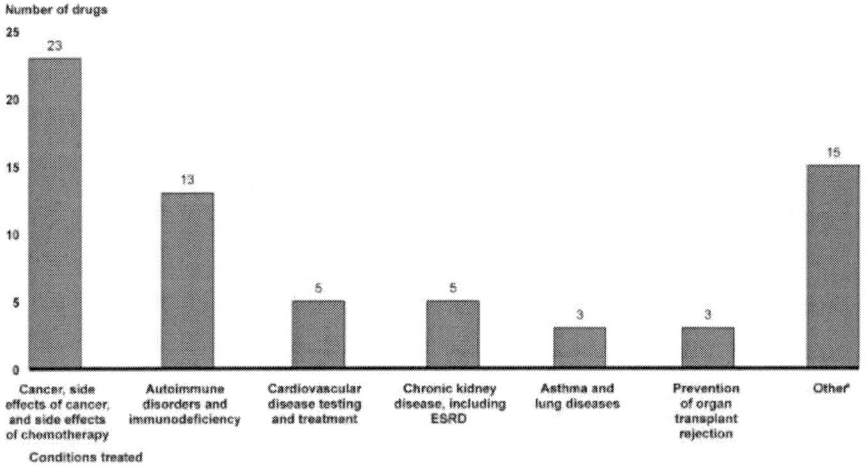

Source: GAO analysis of CMS, NIH, and drug manufacturer data.

Notes: The sum of the high-expenditure Medicare Part B drugs exceeds 55 because some drugs were used to treat more than one type of condition.

[a] Other includes conditions such as wet age-related macular degeneration, osteoarthritis of the knee, myelodysplastic syndrome, anemia in HIV and uterine fibroid patients, and prevention of influenza, pneumonia, and meningitis.

Figure 1. Conditions Treated by the 55 Highest-Expenditure Medicare Part B Drugs, 2010.

Utilization of High-Expenditure Part B Drugs Ranged from Millions of Beneficiaries for Vaccines to Hundreds for Hemophilia Drugs in 2010

Utilization of the 55 highest-expenditure Part B drugs ranged from over 15 million beneficiaries who received the influenza vaccine to 660 beneficiaries who used factor viii recombinant to treat hemophilia A.[25] Although Epogen to treat beneficiaries with ESRD was Medicare's most expensive Part B drug in 2010, other drugs among the top 55 were used by more beneficiaries, including two vaccines (influenza and pneumococcal). Apart from the vaccines, the greatest number of beneficiaries (891,000) used Lexiscan, which is a chemical stress agent used to test heart function in patients who cannot take a stress test on a treadmill (see table 2).

Table 2. Ten Most Utilized High-Expenditure Medicare Part B Drugs, 2010

Brand name(s)	Condition(s) treated	Utilization (number of unique Medicare beneficiaries)
Influenza Vaccine (various)	Prevent influenza	15,229,920
Pnuemovax 23, Pnu-Imune	Prevent meningitis and pneumonia	1,692,940
Lexiscan	Stress agent for myocardial perfusion imaging	890,920
Venofer	Anemia in chronic kidney disease patients	329,260
Epogen/Procrit (ESRD use)	Anemia in end-stage renal disease (ESRD) patients[a]	323,920
Zemplar	Hyperthyroidism in chronic kidney disease patients	230,700
Reclast	Osteoporosis prevention and treatment; treat Paget's disease of bone	218,060
Avastin	Cancer; wet age-related macular degeneration (AMD)	171,560
Synvisc/Synvisc-One	Osteoarthritis of the knee	168,560
Aloxi	Prevent nausea and vomiting in chemotherapy and surgical patients	164,000

Source: GAO analysis of CMS, FDA, NIH, and drug manufacturer data.
[a]End-stage renal disease (ESRD) is also known as stage 5 chronic kidney disease.

Average Annual per Beneficiary Costs for 55 Highest-Expenditure Medicare Part B Drugs Ranged from over $200,000 to $13 in 2010

We also examined the average annual per beneficiary cost of each drug and found that factor viii recombinant, although used by the smallest number of Medicare beneficiaries, was the most costly drug on an average annual per beneficiary cost basis—the average annual cost was about $217,000 for each beneficiary who used it in 2010 (see table 3). The influenza vaccines had the lowest average annual per beneficiary cost ($13). The high average annual per beneficiary cost for factor viii recombinant drugs results in part from the complexity of the production process; consequently, even having several brand names available has not reduced the average annual per beneficiary cost for this drug. Remodulin and Ventavis follow with average annual per beneficiary costs of about $131,000 and $84,000, respectively; both are used to treat pulmonary hypertension (high blood pressure in the lungs due to narrowing of the pulmonary arteries). Primacor, at an average annual per beneficiary cost of about $63,000, is used to treat acute decompensated heart failure (a type of acute heart failure). Apart from these four drugs, no drug cost more than $26,000 per beneficiary per year in 2010.

Table 3. Ten High-Expenditure Medicare Part B Drugs with Highest Average Annual Per Beneficiary Cost, 2010

Brand name(s)	Condition(s) treated	Classification	Average annual cost per beneficiary (dollars)
Factor viii recombinant (various)	Hemophilia A	Biological	$216,833
Remodulin	Pulmonary arterial hypertension	Drug	130,772
Ventavis	Pulmonary arterial hypertension	Drug	84,205
Primacor, Primacor in Dextrose	Acute decompensated heart failure	Drug	62,790
Erbitux	Cancer	Biological	25,898
Dacogen	Myelodysplastic syndrome	Drug	25,858
Herceptin	Cancer	Biological	25,797
Vidaza	Myelodysplastic syndrome	Drug	22,957
Sandostatin Lar Depot	Acromegaly, diarrhea, and flushing caused by cancerous tumors and vasoactive intestinal peptide secreting adenomas	Drug	22,748
Velcade	Cancer	Drug	19,667

Source: GAO analysis of CMS, FDA, NIH, and drug manufacturer data.

Most Changes in Expenditures, Utilization, and Price from 2008 to 2010 Were Increases

Expenditures for drugs generally increased from 2008 to 2010, although some decreased. Medicare expenditures for 42 of the 55 most expensive Part B drugs increased from 2008 to 2010, while 12 decreased.[26] Changes in Medicare expenditures from 2008 to 2010 for the 55 highest-expenditure Part B drugs in 2010 ranged from a 9,550 percent increase to a 40 percent decrease.[27] Utilization also generally increased from 2008 to 2010. The drugs that showed the greatest increases in expenditures were Lexiscan (9,550 percent), Treanda (7,440 percent), Privigen (836 percent), Reclast (141 percent), and Myfortic (107 percent); these drugs also showed the greatest increases in utilization (see table 4). Enclosure V provides information on the 55 highest-expenditure Medicare Part B drugs by changes in expenditures, utilization, and price.

The first four of these drugs had been approved by FDA in 2007 or early 2008, and it took some months for their use to spread.[28] Also, in late 2008 and 2009 Reclast was approved for additional uses, such as for the treatment of osteoporosis in men.

Table 4. Ten High-Expenditure Part B Drugs with Largest Changes in Expenditures, Utilization, and Average Price from 2008 to 2010

Change in expenditures, 2008-2010[a]		Change in utilization, 2008-2010		Change in average price, 2008-2010[b]	
Brand name(s)	Percent change	Brand name(s)	Percent change	Brand name(s)	Percent change
Lexiscan	9,550.4%	Lexiscan	11,008.7%	Ventavis	51.5%
Treanda	7,440.2	Treanda	3,271.4	Pneumovax 23, Pnu-Imune	36.0
Privigen	836.3	Privigen	381.1	Myfortic	22.0
Reclast	140.7	Reclast	136.8	Hycamtin	17.5
Myfortic	106.9	Myfortic	73.4	Gammagard Liquid	15.4
Primacor, Primacor in Dextrose	94.0	Hectorol	71.1	Doxil	14.1
Ventavis	93.6	Flebogamma, Flebogamma DIF	46.7	Tysabri	12.3
Vidaza	81.9	Orencia	45.4	Vidaza	11.6
Gammagard Liquid	69.2	Vidaza	41.7	Gamunex	11.3
Orencia	66.9	Gamunex	36.7	Xolair	11.2

Source: GAO analysis of CMS and FDA data.

Notes: Our analysis excludes expenditures and utilization in 2008 that were reported using a not otherwise classified code, which may have artificially increased the changes shown for new drugs, including Lexiscan and Treanda.

[a]We removed factor viii recombinant biologicals from our analysis of change in expenditures from 2008-2010 because Medicare claims expenditures for 2008 were lower than values in CMS's Part B National Summary Files and we were not confident that the reported expenditures for 2008 were valid.

[b]The change in price analysis was based on the unweighted average ASP across four quarters in each year, and does not include prices for drugs when supplied through infusion equipment.

Most price changes from 2008 to 2010 were also increases but the range was smaller—from an increase in price of 51 percent to a decrease of 38 percent.[29] Four of the 10 that increased most in expenditures also were among the 10 that increased most in price. Ventavis increased the most (51 percent) followed by Pneumovax 23/ Pnu-Immune (36 percent), the vaccine used to prevent pneumonia.

Medicare Beneficiaries Accounted for the Majority of Total U.S. Spending for Most of the Highest-Expenditure Medicare Part B : Covered Drugs in 2010

Spending on Medicare beneficiaries accounted for the majority of estimated total U.S. spending for 35 of the 55 highest-expenditure Part B drugs in 2010. For 17 of these drugs, Medicare spending accounted for more than two-thirds of total U.S. spending (see table 5). Of the $16.9 billion Medicare spent for the 55 highest-expenditure Part B drugs, $11.0 billion, or 65 percent, was spent on drugs for which spending for Medicare beneficiaries accounted for the majority of total U.S. expenditures.

Enclosure VI provides information on the percentage spent on Medicare beneficiaries for the 55 highest-expenditure Part B drugs.

Treatment of cancer and its side effects, autoimmune disorders and immunodeficiency, and chronic kidney disease were the most common uses of the 35 drugs for which Medicare spending was the majority of U.S. spending. Twenty-nine percent of these 35 drugs were biologicals, compared to 42 percent of all 55 drugs.

Agency Comments

CMS provided us with technical comments, which we incorporated as appropriate.

James C. Cosgrove
Director,
Health Care

Table 5. High-Expenditure Medicare Part B Drugs for Which Spending on Medicare Beneficiaries Exceeded Two-thirds of Total U.S. Spending, 2010

2010 rank by total Medicare expenditures	Brand name(s)	Condition(s) treated	Spending on Medicare beneficiaries (dollars in millions)	Spending on total U.S. insured population (dollars in millions)	Percentage spent on Medicare beneficiaries (percent)
47	Myfortic	Prevent transplant kidney rejection; treat Crohn's disease	$80	$86	92.2%
18	Prograf	Prevent transplant organ rejection; treat fistulizing Crohn's disease	267	290	92.1
52	Brovana	Symptoms of chronic obstructive pulmonary disease	70	77	91.3
22	Pulmicort	Prevent wheezing, shortness of breath, and troubled breathing in asthma and lung disease patients	245	273	89.6
33	Aranesp (ESRD use)	Anemia in end-stage renal disease (ESRD) patients[a]	162	182	88.7
45	Primacor, Primacor in Dextrose	Acute decompensated heart failure	87	101	85.6
40	Cellcept	Prevent transplant organ rejection; treat Crohn's disease	113	133	84.9
1	Epogen/Procrit (ESRD use)	Anemia in ESRD patients	2,000	2,381	84.0

Table 5. (Continued)

2010 rank by total Medicare expenditures	Brand name(s)	Condition(s) treated	Spending on Medicare beneficiaries (dollars in millions)	Spending on total U.S. insured population (dollars in millions)	Percentage spent on Medicare beneficiaries (percent)
14	Zemplar	Hyperthyroidism in chronic kidney disease patients	324	389	83.3
3	Lucentis	Wet age-related macular degeneration (AMD)	1,180	1,486	79.5
44	Dacogen	Myelodysplastic syndrome	100	130	77.1
28	Vidaza	Myelodysplastic syndrome	187	245	76.3
48	Ventavis	Pulmonary arterial hypertension	79	104	76.1
19	Venofer	Anemia in chronic kidney disease patients	257	350	73.5
8	Epogen/Procrit (non-ESRD use)	Anemia in chemotherapy and HIV patients; prevent blood loss in surgical patients	443	609	72.7
42	Hectorol	Hyperthyroidism in chronic kidney disease patients	105	150	69.8
7	Aranesp (non-ESRD use)	Anemia in chemotherapy patients	504	755	66.7

Source: GAO analysis of CMS, FDA, NIH, drug manufacturer, and IMS Health data.

[a] End-stage renal disease (ESRD) is also known as stage 5 chronic kidney disease.

Enclosure I

General Information on the 55 Highest-Expenditure Medicare Part B Drugs, 2010

Brand name(s)	Drug description	Healthcare Common Procedure Classification System (HCPCS) code(s)[a]	Classification	Condition(s) treated
Abraxane	Paclitaxel protein bound	J9264	Drug	Cancer
Alimta	Pemetrexed injection	J9305	Drug	Cancer
Aloxi	Palonosetron HCl	J2469	Drug	Prevent nausea and vomiting in chemotherapy and surgical patients
Aranesp (non-ESRD use)[b]	Darbepoetin alfa, non-ESRD	J0881	Biological	Anemia in chemotherapy patients
Aranesp (ESRD use)	Darbepoetin alfa, ESRD	J0882	Biological	Anemia in end-stage renal disease (ESRD) patients
Avastin	Bevacizumab injection	C9257, J9035, Q2024	Biological	Cancer; wet age-related macular degeneration (AMD)
Botox	OnabotulinumtoxinA injection	J0585	Biological	Various conditions
Brovana	Arformoterol non-comp unit	J7605	Drug	Symptoms of chronic obstructive pulmonary disease
Cellcept	Mycophenolate mofetil oral	J7517	Drug	Prevent transplant organ rejection; treat Crohn's disease
Dacogen	Decitabine injection	J0894	Drug	Myelodysplastic syndrome
Doxil	Doxorubicin HCl liposome injection	J9001	Drug	Cancer
Eligard, Lupron Depot, Lupron Depot-PED	Leuprolide acetate suspension	J9217	Drug	Prostate cancer; various other conditions
Eloxatin	Oxaliplatin	J9263	Drug	Cancer

Enclosure I. (Continued)

Brand name(s)	Drug description	Healthcare Common Procedure Classification System (HCPCS) code(s)[a]	Classification	Condition(s) treated
Epogen/Procrit (ESRD use)	Epoetin alfa, ESRD	Q4081	Biological	Anemia in ESRD patients
Epogen/Procrit (non-ESRD use)	Epoetin alfa, non-ESRD	J0885	Biological	Anemia in chemotherapy and HIV patients; prevent blood loss in surgical patients
Erbitux	Cetuximab injection	J9055	Biological	Cancer
Faslodex	Fulvestrant injection	J9395	Drug	Cancer
Flebogamma, Flebogamma DIF	Immune Globulin Intravenous (Human)	J1572	Biological	Primary immunodeficiency
Gammagard Liquid	Immune Globulin Intravenous (Human)	J1569	Biological	Primary humoral immunodeficiency; multifocal motor neuropathy
Gamunex	Immune Globulin Intravenous (Human)	J1561	Biological	Primary humoral immunodeficiency; chronic inflammatory demyelinating polyneuropathy; idiopathic thrombocytopenic purpura
Gemzar	Gemcitabine HCl injection	J9201	Drug	Cancer
Hectorol	Doxercalciferol injection	J1270	Drug	Hyperthyroidism in chronic kidney disease patients
Herceptin	Trastuzumab injection	J9355	Biological	Cancer
Hyalgan, Supartz	Solution of sodium hyaluronate	J7321	Drug	Osteoarthritis of the knee
Hycamtin	Topotecan injection	J9350, J9351	Drug	Cancer
Lexiscan	Regadenoson injection	C9244, J2785	Drug	Stress agent for myocardial perfusion imaging

Brand name(s)	Drug description	Healthcare Common Procedure Classification System (HCPCS) code(s)a	Classification	Condition(s) treated
Lucentis	Ranibizumab injection	J2778	Biological	Wet AMD
Myfortic	Mycophenolic acid	J7518	Drug	Prevent transplant kidney rejection; treat Crohn's disease
Neulasta	Injection, pegfilgrastim 6mg	J2505	Biological	Prevent infection in chemotherapy patients
Neupogen	Filgrastim injection, 300 and 480 mcg	J1440, J1441	Biological	Prevent infection in cancer, bone marrow transplant, chronic neutropenia, and HIV patients; prepare blood for leukapheresis in chemotherapy patients
Orencia	Abatacept injection	J0129	Biological	Rheumatoid arthritis
Pneumovax 23, Pnu-Imune	Pneumococcal vaccine	90732	Biological	Prevent meningitis and pneumonia
Primacor, Primacor in Dextrose	Milrinone lactate 5 mg injection	J2260	Drug	Acute decompensated heart failure
Privigen	Immune Globulin Intravenous (Human)	J1459, Q4097	Biological	Primary humoral immunodeficiency; chronic immune thrombocytopenic purpura
Prograf	Tacrolimus oral per 1 MG	J7507	Drug	Prevent organ transplant rejection; treat fistulizing Crohn's disease
Pulmicort	Budesonide non-comp unit	J7626	Drug	Prevent wheezing, shortness of breath, and troubled breathing in asthma and lung disease patients
Reclast	Zoledronic acid	J3488	Drug	Osteoporosis prevention and treatment; treat Paget'sdisease of bone
Remicade	Infliximab injection	J1745	Biological	Various autoimmune disorders
Remodulin	Treprostinil injection	J3285	Drug	Pulmonary arterial hypertension

Enclosure I. (Continued)

Brand name(s)	Drug description	Healthcare Common Procedure Classification System (HCPCS) code(s)[a]	Classification	Condition(s) treated
Rituxan	Rituximab injection	J9310	Biological	Cancer; rheumatoid arthritis
Sandostatin Lar Depot	Octreotide injection, depot	J2353	Drug	Acromegaly; diarrhea and flushing caused by carcinoid tumors and vasoactive intestinal peptide secreting adenomas
Synvisc, Synvisc-One	Hylan GF 20	J7322, J7325	Drug	Osteoarthritis of the knee
Taxotere	Docetaxel injection	J9170, J9171	Drug	Cancer
Treanda	Bendamustine HCl injection	C9243, J9033	Drug	Cancer
Tysabri	Natalizumab injection	J2323	Biological	Multiple sclerosis; Crohn's disease
Various brand names	Influenza vaccine	90655, 90656, 90657, 90658, 90662, Q2035, Q2036, Q2037, Q2038	Biological	Prevent influenza
Various brand names	Factor viii recombinant	J7192	Biological	Hemophilia A
Various brand names	Immune globulin, powder	J1566	Biological	Primary defective antibody synthesis; primary immunodeficiency diseases; B-cell chronic lymphocytic leukemia; idiopathic thrombocytopenic purpura; Kawasaki syndrome
Velcade	Bortezomib injection	J9041	Drug	Cancer
Venofer	Iron sucrose injection	J1756	Drug	Iron deficiency anemia in chronic kidney disease patients
Ventavis	Iloprost non-comp unit dose	Q4074, Q4080	Drug	Pulmonary arterial hypertension
Vidaza	Azacitidine injection	J9025	Drug	Myelodysplastic syndrome
Xolair	Omalizumab injection	J2357	Drug	Asthma

Brand name(s)	Drug description	Healthcare Common Procedure Classification System (HCPCS) code(s)[a]	Classification	Condition(s) treated
Zemplar	Paricalcitol	J2501	Drug	Hyperparathyroidism in chronic kidney disease patients
Zometa	Zoledronic acid	J3487	Drug	High calcium levels and bone disease in cancer patients

Source: GAO analysis of CMS, FDA, NIH, and drug manufacturer data.

[a] Healthcare Common Procedure Coding System (HCPCS) is a standard coding system developed to ensure that health care claims are processed in an orderly and consistent manner by Medicare and other health insurance programs.

[b] End-stage renal disease (ESRD) is also known as stage 5 chronic kidney disease.

ENCLOSURE II

Fifty-Five Highest-Expenditure Medicare B Drugs Ranked by Total Expenditures, Utilization, and Average Annual Per Beneficiary Cost, 2010

	Total expenditures, 2010		Beneficiary utilization, 2010		Per beneficiary cost, 2010	
Brand name(s)	**Total (dollars in millions)**	**Rank by total Medicare expenditures**	**Number of unique beneficiaries**	**Rank by beneficiary utilization**	**Average annual cost per beneficiary (dollars)**	**Rank by annual cost per beneficiary**
Epogen/Procrit (ESRD use)[a]	$2,000	1	323,920	5	$6,175	32
Rituxan	1,302	2	67,520	21	19,281	11
Lucentis	1,180	3	115,760	17	10,196	27
Avastin	1,130	4	171,560	8	6,585	31

Enclosure II. (Continued)

	Total expenditures, 2010		Beneficiary utilization, 2010		Per beneficiary cost, 2010	
Brand name(s)	**Total (dollars in millions)**	**Rank by total Medicare expenditures**	**Number of unique beneficiaries**	**Rank by beneficiary utilization**	**Average annual cost per beneficiary (dollars)**	**Rank by annual cost per beneficiary**
Remicade	900	5	59,640	23	15,084	20
Neulasta	888	6	98,460	18	9,015	28
Aranesp (non-ESRD use)	504	7	137,980	14	3,651	38
Epogen/Procrit (non-ESRD use)	443	8	154,720	12	2,862	40
Alimta	394	9	20,740	31	18,990	13
Taxotere	387	10	44,560	28	8,690	29
Herceptin	375	11	14,540	35	25,797	7
Zometa	350	12	90,260	19	3,881	37
Gemzar	349	13	44,660	27	7,820	30
Zemplar	324	14	230,700	6	1,406	46
Velcade	297	15	15,120	34	19,667	10
Eloxatin	290	16	27,260	30	10,649	26
Erbitux	275	17	10,620	38	25,898	5
Prograf	267	18	61,280	22	4,351	35
Venofer	257	19	329,260	4	782	50
Eligard, Lupron Depot, Lupron Depot-PED	256	20	159,700	11	1,600	44
Reclast	245	21	218,060	7	1,122	48
Pulmicort	245	22	142,440	13	1,717	43
Orencia	240	23	20,040	32	11,953	24
Sandostatin Lar Depot	210	24	9,220	40	22,748	9
Influenza Vaccine (various)	193	25	15,229,920	1	13	55
Gammagard Liquid	191	26	10,880	37	17,543	15

	Total expenditures, 2010		Beneficiary utilization, 2010		Per beneficiary cost, 2010	
Brand name(s)	**Total (dollars in millions)**	**Rank by total Medicare expenditures**	**Number of unique beneficiaries**	**Rank by beneficiary utilization**	**Average annual cost per beneficiary (dollars)**	**Rank by annual cost per beneficiary**
Aloxi	190	27	164,000	10	1,161	47
Vidaza	187	28	8,160	43	22,957	8
Lexiscan	181	29	890,920	3	204	53
Treanda	181	30	9,440	39	19,218	12
Neupogen	171	31	53,020	24	3,232	39
Remodulin	170	32	1,300	53	130,772	2
Aranesp (ESRD use)	162	33	31,800	29	5,086	34
Factor viii recombinant (various)	143	34	660	55	216,833	1
Gamunex	142	35	8,420	42	16,862	17
Tysabri	139	36	7,340	46	18,978	14
Botox	136	37	67,860	20	2,008	42
Abraxane	128	38	7,520	44	16,989	16
Synvisc, Synvisc-One	126	39	168,560	9	746	51
Cellcept	113	40	48,740	25	2,322	41
Xolair	110	41	7,420	45	14,774	21
Hectorol	105	42	127,440	16	820	49
Doxil	103	43	9,160	41	11,195	25
Dacogen	100	44	3,860	51	25,858	6
Primacor, Primacor in Dextrose	87	45	1,380	52	62,790	4
Immune globulin, powder (various)	80	46	6,120	47	13,139	22
Myfortic	80	47	19,280	33	4,131	36
Ventavis	79	48	940	54	84,205	3
Privigen	78	49	5,100	49	15,335	19

Enclosure II. (Continued)

	Total expenditures, 2010		Beneficiary utilization, 2010		Per beneficiary cost, 2010	
Brand name(s)	**Total (dollars in millions)**	**Rank by total Medicare expenditures**	**Number of unique beneficiaries**	**Rank by beneficiary utilization**	**Average annual cost per beneficiary (dollars)**	**Rank by annual cost per beneficiary**
Hycamtin	75	50	5,840	48	12,768	23
Pnuemovax-23, Pnu-Imune	73	51	1,692,940	2	43	54
Brovana	70	52	45,920	26	1,528	45
Faslodex	70	53	11,700	36	5,959	33
Hyalgan, Supartz	69	54	132,620	15	520	52
Flebogamma, Flebogamma DIF	63	55	4,020	50	15,684	18

Source: GAO analysis of CMS and FDA data.

[a] End-stage renal disease (ESRD) is also known as stage 5 chronic kidney disease.

ENCLOSURE III

High-Expenditure Medicare Part B Drugs with Orphan Marketing Exclusivity during 2008 to 2010

2010 rank by total Medicare expenditures	Brand name(s) of orphan drug	Orphan exclusivity in 2008-2010	Orphan exclusivity start date(s) and indication(s), 2008-present	Year(s) of orphan exclusivity expiration
2	Rituxan	Yes	02-18-2010 Treatment of patients previously untreated for CD20-positive chronic lymphocytic leukemia in combination with fludarbine and cyclophosphamide 04-19-2011 For the use of Rituxan (rituximab) in combination with glucocorticoids for the treatment of patients with Wegener's Granulomatosis and Microscopic Polyangiitis	2017, 2018
4	Avastin	Yes	05-05-2009 Treatment of glioblastoma with progressive disease following prior therapy 07-31-2009 Treatment of renal cell carcinoma in combination with interferon alfa	2016
5	Remicade	Yes	05-19-2006 For reducing signs and symptoms and inducing and maintaining clinical remission in pediatric patients with moderately to severely active Crohn's disease who have had an inadequate response to conventional therapy; 09-23-2011 For reducing signs and symptoms and inducing and maintaining clinical remission in pediatric patients 6 years of age and older with moderately to severely active ulcerative colitis who have had an inadequate response to conventional therapy	2013, 2018
9	Alimta	Yes	02-04-2004 Treatment of patients with malignant pleural mesothelioma whose disease is either unresectable or who are otherwise not candidates for curative surgery	2011

Enclosure III. (Continued)

2010 rank by total Medicare expenditures	Brand name(s) of orphan drug	Orphan exclusivity in 2008-2010	Orphan exclusivity start date(s) and indication(s), 2008-present	Year(s) of orphan exclusivity expiration
11	Herceptin	Yes	10-20-2010 Treatment of patients with humana epidermal growth factor receptor 2 overexpressing metastatic gastric or gastroesophageal junction adenocarcinoma, who have not received prior treatment for metastatic disease	2017
12	Zometa	Yes	08-20-2001 Treatment of hypercalcemia of malignancy	2008
15	Velcade	Yes	05-13-2003 Treatment of multiple myeloma patients who have received at least two prior therapies and have demonstrated disease progression on the last therapy 12-08-2006 Treatment of patients with mantile cell lymphoma who have received at least one prior therapy.	2010, 2013
17	Erbitux	Yes	03-01-2006 For use in combination with radiation therapy, for the treatment of locally or regionally advanced squamous cell carcinoma of the head and neck (SCCHN) and for use as a single agent for the treatment of patients with recurrent or metastatic SCCHN for whom prior platinum-based therapy has failed	2013
18	Prograf	Yes	03-29-2006 Prophylaxis of organ rejection in patients receiving allogenic heart transplants	2013
28	Vidaza	Yes	05-19-2004 Treatment of patients with the following myelodysplastic syndrome subtypes: refractory anemia or refractory anemia with ringed sideroblasts (if accompanied by neutropenia or thrombocytopenia and requiring transfusions), refractory anemia with excess blasts, refractory anemia with excess blasts in transformation, and chronic myelomonocytic leukemia	2011
30	Treanda	Yes	03-20-2008 Treatment of patients with chronic lymphocytic leukemia	2015

2010 rank by total Medicare expenditures	Brand name(s) of orphan drug	Orphan exclusivity in 2008-2010	Orphan exclusivity start date(s) and indication(s), 2008-present	Year(s) of orphan exclusivity expiration
32	Remodulin	Yes	05-21-2002 Treatment of pulmonary arterial hypertension	2009
35	Gamunex	Yes	09-12-2008 Treatment of chronic inflammatory demyelinating polyneuropathy to improve neuromuscular disability and impairment and for maintenance therapy to prevent relapse	2015
43	Doxil	Yes	05-17-2007 For use in combination with bortezomib for the treatment of patients with multiple myeloma who have not previously received bortezomib and have at least one prior therapy	2014
44	Dacogen	Yes	05-02-2006 for treatment of patients with myelodysplastic syndromes (MDS) including previously treated and untreated, de novo and secondary MDS of all French-American-British subtypes (refractory anemia, refractory anemia with ringed sideroblasts, refractory anemia with excess blasts, refractory anemia with excess blasts in transformation, and chronic myelomonocytic leukemia) and intermediate-1, intermediate-2, and high-risk International Prognostic Scoring System groups	2013
48	Ventavis	Yes	12-29-2004 Treatment of pulmonary arterial hypertension in patients with symptoms of moderate or severe heart failure	2011

Source: GAO analysis of CMS and FDA data.

Note: Upon approval by FDA for specific orphan indications, orphan drugs receive marketing exclusivity for a period of 7 years. Other drugs in our analysis have been designated as orphan drugs by FDA, but did not have orphan marketing exclusivity at any point during 2008 to 2010. In addition to the drugs listed above, one drug in our analysis, Gammagard Liquid, has an orphan exclusivity start date of June 22, 2012, for an indication of maintenance therapy to improve muscle strength and disability in adult patients with multifocal motor neuropathy.

Enclosure IV

Nine of the 55 Highest-Expenditure Medicare Part B Drugs with Generic Products Approved

2010 rank by total Medicare expenditures	Brand name(s)	Generic version approved by FDA	Date of firstgeneric approval
10	Taxotere	Yes	3/8/2011[a]
13	Gemzar	Yes	11/15/2010
14	Zemplar	Yes	7/27/2011[a]
16	Eloxatin	Yes	8/7/2009
18	Prograf	Yes	8/10/2009
22	Pulmicort	Yes	11/18/2008
40	Cellcept	Yes	7/29/2008
45	Primacor, Primacor in Dextrose	Yes (however, some versions of this drug are listed as discontinued)	5/28/2002
50	Hycamtin	Yes	11/29/2010

Source: GAO analysis of CMS and FDA data.

Notes: The date of first generic approval does not necessarily indicate the date on which a generic version was available on the market.

[a] A generic version was approved after 2010, the most recent year of our analysis.

ENCLOSURE V

Fifty-Five Highest-Expenditure Medicare Part B Drugs Ranked Highest to Lowest by Change in Expenditures, Change in Number of Beneficiaries, and Change in Average Price, 2008 to 2010

Change in expenditures, 2008-2010		Change in beneficiaries, 2008-2010		Change in average price, 2008-2010[a]	
Brand name(s)	Percent change	Brand name(s)	Percent change	Brand name(s)	Percent change
Lexiscan	9,550.4%	Lexiscan	11,008.7%	Ventavis	51.5%
Treanda	7,440.2	Treanda	3,271.4	Pneumovax 23, Pnu-Imune	36.0
Privigen	836.3	Privigen	381.1	Myfortic	22.0
Reclast	140.7	Reclast	136.8	Hycamtin	17.5
Myfortic	106.9	Myfortic	73.4	Gammagard Liquid	15.4
Primacor, Primacor in Dextrose	94.0	Hectorol	71.1	Doxil	14.1
Ventavis	93.6	Flebogamma, Flebogamma DIF	46.7	Tysabri	12.3
Vidaza	81.9	Orencia	45.4	Vidaza	11.6
Gammagard Liquid	69.2	Vidaza	41.7	Gamunex	11.3
Orencia	66.9	Gamunex	36.7	Xolair	11.2
Gamunex	66.5	Velcade	35.5	Velcade	11.1
Flebogamma, Flebogamma DIF	62.3	Tysabri	34.9	Neulasta	11.1
Velcade	56.9	Gammagard Liquid	32.0	Rituxan	11.0
Lucentis	56.6	Alimta	30.3	Hectorol	10.6
Xolair	55.8	Lucentis	29.6	Herceptin	10.5
Tysabri	50.5	Brovana	28.8	Gemzar	10.0
Alimta	49.7	Synvisc, Synvisc-One	27.8	Dacogen	9.7
Brovana	48.0	Primacor, Primacor in Dextrose	27.8	Alimta	9.5
Hectorol	47.1	Venofer	27.0	Taxotere[b]	9.2
Remodulin	40.7	Sandostatin Lar Depot	22.9	Aloxi	8.6

Enclosure V. (Continued)

Change in expenditures, 2008-2010		Change in beneficiaries, 2008-2010		Change in average price, 2008-2010[a]	
Brand name(s)	Percent change	Brand name(s)	Percent change	Brand name(s)	Percent change
Synvisc, Synvisc-One	36.0	Remodulin	22.6	Flebogamma, Flebogamma DIF	7.7
Venofer	33.4	Xolair	20.5	Sandostatin Lar Depot	7.1
Sandostatin Lar Depot	29.2	Prograf	19.5	Immune globulin, powder (various)	6.9
Faslodex	27.7	Abraxane	16.8	Abraxane	6.4
Pneumovax 23, Pnu-Imune	26.1	Avastin	14.0	Orencia	6.3
Dacogen	24.6	Zemplar	8.6	Remicade	6.3
Eligard, Lupron Depot, Lupron Depot-PED	24.3	Aloxi	7.2	Brovana	6.0
Herceptin	22.1	Botox	6.7	Epogen/Procrit (non-ESRD use)[c]	5.9
Botox	20.8	Epogen/Procrit (ESRD use)	6.0	Epogen/Procrit (ESRD use)	5.8
Abraxane	20.4	Influenza Vaccine (various)	5.6	Pulmicort	5.5
Aloxi	18.7	Herceptin	4.3	Zometa	4.7
Doxil	16.9	Zometa	4.3	Privigen	3.8
Avastin	15.5	Cellcept	2.8	Botox	3.4
Epogen/Procrit (ESRD use)	11.6	Rituxan	2.8	Lexiscan[d]	2.8
Rituxan	8.7	Eloxatin	0.5	Reclast	2.6
Remicade	8.6	Aranesp (ESRD use)	0.0	Venofer	2.4
Gemzar	8.5	Eligard, Lupron Depot, Lupron Depot-PED	-0.5	Factor viii recombinant (various)	2.1
Neulasta	6.5	Gemzar	-0.8	Faslodex	1.6
Zometa	6.0	Faslodex	-1.5	Aranesp (non-ESRD use)	1.1
Hycamtin	5.1	Remicade	-2.3	Aranesp (ESRD use)	1.1

Change in expenditures, 2008-2010		Change in beneficiaries, 2008-2010		Change in average price, 2008-2010[a]	
Brand name(s)	Percent change	Brand name(s)	Percent change	Brand name(s)	Percent change
Neupogen	3.8	Doxil	-2.3	Remodulin	1.0
Prograf	0.3	Dacogen	-3.0	Avastin[e]	1.0
Influenza Vaccine (various)	-0.6	Taxotere	-4.1	Erbitux	-0.1
Erbitux	-2.7	Neulasta	-4.9	Lucentis	-0.1
Taxotere	-4.2	Pneumovax 23, Pnu-Imune	-5.5	Treanda[d]	-0.4
Epogen/Procrit (non-ESRD use)	-6.4	Neupogen	-5.5	Eligard, Lupron Depot, Lupron Depot-PED	-0.5
Aranesp (ESRD use)	-9.1	Ventavis	-7.8	Zemplar	-7.4
Zemplar	-16.2	Pulmicort	-9.3	Hyalgan, Supartz	-9.0
Pulmicort	-16.5	Hycamtin	-12.0	Prograf	-13.4
Hyalgan, Supartz	-17.4	Hyalgan, Supartz	-12.8	Primacor, Primacor in Dextrose	-17.6
Aranesp (non-ESRD use)	-27.8	Erbitux	-14.4	Cellcept	-38.1
Eloxatin	-39.5	Immune globulin, powder (various)	-32.5	Influenza Vaccine (various)[f]	N/A
Cellcept	-40.3	Aranesp (non-ESRD use)	-33.6	Neupogen[f]	N/A
Factor viii recombinant (various)[g]	N/A	Factor viii recombinant (various)[g]	N/A	Synvisc, Synvisc-One[f]	N/A

Source: GAO analysis of CMS and FDA data.

Notes: Our analysis excludes expenditures and utilization in 2008 that were reported using a not otherwise classified code, which may have had an impact on our analysis of new drugs, including Lexiscan and Treanda.

[a] The change in price analysis was based on the unweighted average ASP across four quarters in each year, and does not include prices for drugs when supplied through infusion equipment.

[b] Our analysis of the change in average price for Taxotere includes an adjustment for a change in dosage between 2008 and 2010.

[c] End-stage renal disease (ESRD) is also known as stage 5 chronic kidney disease.

[d] Our analysis of changes in price for Lexiscan and Treanda only includes changes from 2009-2010 as 2008 ASP information was not available.

[e] Our analysis of Avastin only includes changes in price for Healthcare Common Procedure Classification System (HCPCS) code J9035 due to dosage differences for other codes used to identify Avastin. Code J9035 accounted for the vast majority of Avastin expenditures in 2010.

[f] Change in average price could not be analyzed for the influenza vaccine, Neupogen, or Synvisc/Synvisc-One because the multiple HCPCS codes that are associated with these drugs have different units or dosage amounts.

[g] We removed factor viii recombinant from our analysis of change in expenditures from 2008-2010 because we were not confident that the expenditures for 2008 were valid.

ENCLOSURE VI

Fifty-Five Highest-Expenditure Medicare Part B Drugs by Percentage Spent on Medicare Beneficiaries, 2010

Brand name(s)	Condition(s) treated	Spending on Medicare beneficiaries (dollars in millions)	Spending on total U.S. insured population (dollars in millions)	Percentage spent on Medicare beneficiaries (percent)	2010 rank by total Medicare expenditures
Myfortic	Prevent transplant kidney rejection; treat Crohn's disease	$80	$86	92.2%	47
Prograf	Prevent transplant organ rejection; treat fistulizing Crohn's disease	267	290	92.1	18
Brovana	Symptoms of chronic obstructive pulmonary disease	70	77	91.3	52
Pulmicort	Prevent wheezing, shortness of breath, and troubled breathing in asthma and lung disease patients	245	273	89.6	22
Aranesp (ESRD use)	Anemia in end-stage renal disease (ESRD) patients[a]	162	182	88.7	33

Brand name(s)	Condition(s) treated	Spending on Medicare beneficiaries (dollars in millions)	Spending on total U.S. insured population (dollars in millions)	Percentage spent on Medicare beneficiaries (percent)	2010 rank by total Medicare expenditures
Primacor, Primacor in Dextrose	Acute decompensated heart failure	87	101	85.6	45
Cellcept	Prevent transplant organ rejection; treat Crohn's disease	113	133	84.9	40
Epogen/Procrit (ESRD use)	Anemia in ESRD patients	2,000	2,381	84.0	1
Zemplar	Hyperparathyroidism in chronic kidney disease patients	324	389	83.3	14
Lucentis	Wet age-related macular degeneration (AMD)	1,180	1,486	79.5	3
Dacogen	Myelodysplastic syndrome	100	130	77.1	44
Vidaza	Myelodysplastic syndrome	187	245	76.3	28
Ventavis	Pulmonary arterial hypertension	79	104	76.1	48
Venofer	Iron deficiency anemia in chronic kidney disease patients	257	350	73.5	19
Epogen/Procrit (non-ESRD use)	Anemia in chemotherapy and HIV patients; prevent blood loss in surgical patients	443	609	72.7	8
Hectorol	Hyperthyroidism in chronic kidney disease patients	105	150	69.8	42
Aranesp (non-ESRD use)	Anemia in chemotherapy patients	504	755	66.7	7
Eligard, Lupron Depot, Lupron Depot-PED	Prostate cancer; various other conditions	256	410	62.4	20
Lexiscan	Stress agent for myocardial perfusion imaging	181	299	60.7	29

Enclosure VI. (Continued)

Brand name(s)	Condition(s) treated	Spending on Medicare beneficiaries (dollars in millions)	Spending on total U.S. insured population (dollars in millions)	Percentage spent on Medicare beneficiaries (percent)	2010 rank by total Medicare expenditures
Reclast	Osteoporosis prevention and treatment; treat Paget's disease of bone	245	408	60.0	21
Faslodex	Cancer	70	117	59.6	53
Alimta	Cancer	394	673	58.5	9
Treanda	Cancer	181	313	58.0	30
Velcade	Cancer	297	527	56.5	15
Zometa	High calcium levels and bone disease in cancer patients	350	630	55.6	12
Erbitux	Cancer	275	495	55.5	17
Gemzar	Cancer	349	629	55.5	13
Neupogen	Prevent infection in cancer, bone marrow transplant, chronic neutropenia, and HIV patients; prepare blood for leukapheresis in chemotherapy patients	171	309	55.5	31
Hycamtin	Cancer	75	134	55.5	50
Remodulin	Pulmonary arterial hypertension	170	308	55.1	32
Doxil	Cancer	103	188	54.4	43
Pneumovax 23, Pnu-Imune	Prevent meningitis and pneumonia	73	135	54.2	51
Rituxan	Cancer; rheumatoid arthritis	1,302	2,490	52.3	2

Brand name(s)	Condition(s) treated	Spending on Medicare beneficiaries (dollars in millions)	Spending on total U.S. insured population (dollars in millions)	Percentage spent on Medicare beneficiaries (percent)	2010 rank by total Medicare expenditures
Sandostatin Lar Depot	Acromegaly; diarrhea and flushing caused by carcinoid tumors and vasoactive intestinal peptide secreting adenomas	210	403	52.1	24
Flebogamma, Flebogamma DIF	Primary immunodeficiency	63	124	50.7	55
Avastin	Cancer; wet AMD	1,130	2,527	44.7	4
Abraxane	Cancer	128	289	44.2	38
Hyalgan, Supartz	Osteoarthritis of the knee	69	159	43.4	54
Orencia	Rheumatoid arthritis	240	564	42.4	23
Synvisc, Synvisc-One	Osteoarthritis of the knee	126	314	40.0	39
Neulasta	Prevent infection in chemotherapy patients	888	2,254	39.4	6
Taxotere	Cancer	387	1,041	37.2	10
Privigen	Primary humoral immunodeficiency; chronic immune thrombocytopenic purpura	78	224	34.9	49
Aloxi	Prevent nausea and vomiting in chemotherapy and surgical patients	190	553	34.4	27

Enclosure VI. (Continued)

Brand name(s)	Condition(s) treated	Spending on Medicare beneficiaries (dollars in millions)	Spending on total U.S. insured population (dollars in millions)	Percentage spent on Medicare beneficiaries (percent)	2010 rank by total Medicare expenditures
Immune globulin, powder (various)	Primary defective antibody synthesis; primary immunodeficiency diseases; B-cell chronic lymphocytic leukemia; idiopathic thrombocytopenic purpura; Kawasaki syndrome	80	234	34.4	46
Eloxatin	Cancer	290	868	33.4	16
Influenza Vaccine (various)	Prevent influenza	193	603	32.0	25
Botox	Various conditions	136	429	31.8	37
Herceptin	Cancer	375	1,257	29.8	11
Gamunex	Primary humoral immunodeficiency; chronic inflammatory demyelinating polyneuropathy; idiopathic thrombocytopenic purpura	142	481	29.5	35
Xolair	Asthma	110	374	29.3	41
Remicade	Various autoimmune disorders	900	3,229	27.9	5
Factor viii recombinant (various)	Hemophilia A	143	526	27.2	34

Brand name(s)	Condition(s) treated	Spending on Medicare beneficiaries (dollars in millions)	Spending on total U.S. insured population (dollars in millions)	Percentage spent on Medicare beneficiaries (percent)	2010 rank by total Medicare expenditures
Gammagard Liquid	Primary humoral immunodeficiency; multifocal motor neuropathy	191	770	24.8	26
Tysabri	Multiple sclerosis; Crohn's disease	139	588	23.7	36

Source: GAO analysis of CMS, FDA, NIH, and drug manufacturer data.

[a] End-stage renal disease (ESRD) is also known as stage 5 chronic kidney disease.

End Notes

[1] Medicare Part B covers certain physician, outpatient hospital, laboratory and other services, and medical equipment and supplies. Under certain circumstances, drugs that are usually administered to outpatients may be administered to inpatients and covered by Medicare Part A.

[2] In this report the terms "drugs" refers to chemically synthesized drugs and biologicals unless otherwise specified. Biologicals are products derived from living sources, including humans, animals, and microorganisms.

[3] Medicare Part D is a voluntary program through which Medicare covers outpatient prescription drugs. The estimate of total expenditures includes beneficiary payments for premiums but excludes beneficiary expenditure-sharing.

[4] For each claim type, the CMS National Claims History 5 Percent Sample file contains a random sample of all claims paid by Medicare.

[5] Our ranking of highest-expenditure Part B drugs is a snapshot of total spending in 2010. The list of highest-expenditure Part B drugs will change over time as new drugs enter the market and drug utilization changes. CMS has noted that, while outside the scope of our analysis, several extremely expensive injectable products entered the market during or after 2010, including Provenge, Jevtana, Benlysta, and others.

[6] For the remainder of this report, we use the term Medicare spending to refer to spending by the Medicare program and spending by or on behalf of Medicare beneficiaries.

[7] IMS Health's national claims data base is called the LifeLink Health Plan Claims Database.

[8] TRICARE is the Department of Defense's health care system for active duty and retired uniformed service members and their families.

[9] This check resulted in the removal of one drug (factor viii recombinant) from our 2008 analyses of utilization and expenditures due to low reported expenditures in the 2008 Medicare claims data.

[10] Hemophilia A is a hereditary bleeding disorder caused by a lack of blood clotting factor viii. Without enough factor viii, the blood cannot clot properly to stop bleeding.

[11] Influenza, pneumococcal, and hepatitis B vaccines for certain individuals are covered only under Medicare Part B, regardless of the setting in which they are furnished (for example, even when provided to an inpatient during a hospital stay covered under Medicare Part A). Other vaccines, such as the shingles vaccine, are covered under Medicare Part D.

[12] Erythropoiesis-stimulating agents are used to stimulate the bone marrow to produce red blood cells.

[13] A Medicare supplemental health insurance policy is health insurance sold by private insurers that covers Medicare deductibles and copayments as well as some services that Medicare FFS does not cover.

[14] The prices used to determine payment rates for the vaccines and blood products are updated to reflect current AWPs. For DME infusion drugs, payment is based on the AWP in effect on October 1, 2003.

[15] Part B drugs in the hospital outpatient setting are paid separately if the per day expenditure of the drug exceeds a certain threshold set by CMS each year. In 2010, this threshold was $65 per day.

[16] Orphan drug status is granted by FDA to drugs and biologics that treat rare diseases. FDA provides this designation to medications intended to prevent, diagnose, or treat conditions that affect fewer than 200,000 people in the United States or to those that affect more than

200,000 persons, but whose sponsors have no reasonable expectation of recovering the costs of developing and marketing a treatment drug.

[17] In 2010, Medicare paid for pass-through drugs at 106 percent of ASP. The additional pass-through payment amount for 2010, therefore, was the difference between this amount and the usual payment limit of 104 percent of ASP for non-pass-through drugs in the hospital outpatient setting in 2010.

[18] Patents may be applied for and granted at any time during the development and testing of the drug. As a consequence, a sponsor may have fewer than 20 years to market the drug exclusively under the patent.

[19] Biological products do not have generic equivalents, but biosimilars or follow-on biologics serve a similar function. A biosimilar is a biological product that is highly similar to an already approved biological product, notwithstanding minor differences in clinically inactive components, and for which there are no clinically meaningful differences between the biosimilar and the approved biological product in terms of the safety, purity, and potency.

[20] During this 7-year period, FDA may not approve applications to market other versions of the same drug for the same diseases or conditions. See 21 U.S.C. § 360cc. This period can run concurrently with a patent term or not. It is granted for FDA-approved uses of a drug. Other benefits of orphan status may include a tax credit of 50 percent of the cost of conducting human clinical testing, research grants for clinical testing of new therapies to treat orphan diseases, and exemption from the fees that are typically charged when sponsors submit NDAs for FDA's review.

[21] Rtiuxan, Avastin, Remicade, and Almita had orphan drug marketing exclusivity.

[22] Epogen/Procrit for the treatment of anemia in non-ESRD patients was the eighth most expensive Part B drug in 2010. ESRD is also known as stage 5 chronic kidney disease.

[23] Beginning in 2011, CMS implemented bundled payments for drugs and services to Medicare dialysis facilities, which treat ESRD, in part to discourage excessive use of separately billable drugs such as Epogen. Since then, Medicare has not paid separately for 5 of the 55 drugs in our analysis when they are used to treat chronic kidney disease: Epogen/Procrit, Aranesp, Zemplar, Venofer, and Hectorol.

[24] Off-label use refers to using a drug for a condition or patient population for which the drug has not been approved by FDA or in a manner that is inconsistent with the information found in the drug's labeling that has been approved by FDA. We did not separate expenditures on Avastin for cancer and for wet AMD.

[25] Hemophilia A is a hereditary bleeding disorder caused by a lack of blood clotting factor viii. Without enough factor viii, the blood cannot clot properly to stop bleeding.

[26] We removed factor viii recombinant from our analysis of change in expenditures from 2008-2010 because we were not confident that the expenditures for 2008 were valid.

[27] Percent change in expenditures is calculated as the difference between 2010 and 2008 expenditures as a percentage of 2008 expenditures.

[28] Our analysis excludes expenditures and utilization in 2008 that were reported using a not otherwise classified code, which may have artificially increased the changes shown for new drugs, including Lexiscan and Treanda.

[29] Percent change in average price is calculated as the difference between 2010 and 2008 average prices as a percentage of the 2008 average price.

In: Medicare Part B
Editor: Ricardo Visser

ISBN: 978-1-62808-097-1

Chapter 3

MEDICARE PRIMER*

Patricia A. Davis, Scott R. Talaga, Cliff Binder, Jim Hahn, Suzanne M. Kirchhoff, Paulette C. Morgan and Sibyl Tilson

SUMMARY

Medicare is a federal program that pays for covered health care services of qualified beneficiaries. It was established in 1965 under Title XVIII of the Social Security Act to provide health insurance to individuals 65 and older, and has been expanded over the years to include permanently disabled individuals under 65. Medicare, which consists of four parts (A-D), covers hospitalizations, physician services, prescription drugs, skilled nursing facility care, home health visits, and hospice care, among other services.

Generally, individuals are eligible for Medicare if they or their spouse worked for at least 40 quarters in Medicare-covered employment, are 65 years old, and are a citizen or permanent resident of the United States. Individuals may also qualify for coverage if they are a younger person with a permanent disability, have End-Stage Renal disease (permanent kidney failure requiring dialysis or transplant), or have amyotrophic lateral sclerosis (ALS, Lou Gehrig's disease). The program is administered by the Centers for Medicare & Medicaid Services (CMS),

* This is an edited, reformatted and augmented version of Congressional Research Service, Publication No. R40425, dated February 28, 2013.

and by private entities that contract with CMS to provide claims processing, auditing, and quality oversight services.

In FY2013, the program will cover approximately 52 million persons (43 million aged and 9 million disabled) at a total cost of about $598 billion. Spending under the program (except for a portion of administrative costs) is considered mandatory spending and is not subject to the appropriations process. Services provided under Parts A and B (also referred to as "traditional Medicare") are generally paid directly by the government on a "fee-for-service" basis, using different prospective payment systems or fee schedules. Under Parts C and D, private insurers are paid a monthly "capitated" amount to provide enrollees with at least a minimum standard benefit. Medicare is required to pay for all covered services provided to eligible persons, so long as specific criteria are met.

Since 1965, the Medicare program has undergone considerable change. For example, during the 111th Congress, the Patient Protection and Affordable Care Act (ACA; P.L. 111-148 and P.L. 111- 152) made numerous changes to the Medicare program that modify provider reimbursements, provide incentives to increase the quality and efficiency of care, and enhance certain Medicare benefits. However, in the absence of further congressional action, the Medicare program is expected to be unsustainable in the long run. The Hospital Insurance (Part A) trust fund has been estimated to become insolvent in 2024. Additionally, although the Supplementary Medical Insurance (Parts B and D) trust fund is financed in large part through federal general revenues and cannot become insolvent, associated spending growth is expected to put increasing strains on the country's competing priorities. As such, Medicare is expected to be a high-priority issue in the 113th Congress, and Congress may consider a variety of Medicare reform options ranging from further modifications of provider payment mechanisms to redesigning the entire program.

INTRODUCTION

Medicare is a federal program that pays for covered health care services of qualified beneficiaries. It was established in 1965 under Title XVIII of the Social Security Act to provide health insurance to individuals 65 and older, and has been expanded over the years to include permanently disabled individuals under 65. The program is administered by the Centers for Medicare & Medicaid Services (CMS),[1] within the U.S. Department of Health and Human Services (HHS).

Medicare consists of four distinct parts:

- Part A (Hospital Insurance, or HI) covers inpatient hospital services, skilled nursing care, hospice care, and some home health services. The HI trust fund is mainly funded by a dedicated payroll tax of 2.9% of earnings, shared equally between employers and workers.
- Part B (Supplementary Medical Insurance, or SMI) covers physician services, outpatient services, and some home health and preventive services. The SMI trust fund is funded through beneficiary premiums (set at 25% of estimated program costs for the aged) and general revenues (the remaining amount, approximately 75%).
- Part C (Medicare Advantage, or MA) is a private plan option for beneficiaries that covers all Parts A and B services, except hospice. Individuals choosing to enroll in Part C must also enroll in Part B. Part C is funded through the HI and SMI trust funds.
- Part D covers outpatient prescription drug benefits. Funding is included in the SMI trust fund and is financed through beneficiary premiums, general revenues, and state transfer payments.

Medicare serves approximately one in six Americans and virtually all of the population aged 65 and over. In 2013, the program will cover an estimated 52 million persons (43 million aged and 9 million disabled). The Congressional Budget Office (CBO)[2] estimates that total Medicare spending in 2013 will be about $598 billion; of this amount, close to $580 billion will be spent on benefits. Almost a third of Medicare benefit spending is for hospital inpatient and outpatient services (see Figure 1). CBO also estimates that federal Medicare spending (after deduction of beneficiary premiums and other offsetting receipts) will be close to $508 billion in 2013, accounting for about 14% of total federal spending and 3% of GDP. Medicare is required to pay for all covered services provided to eligible persons, so long as specific criteria are met. Spending under the program (except for a portion of administrative costs) is considered mandatory spending and is not subject to the appropriations process.

Medicare is expected to be a high-priority issue in the 113th Congress. The program has a significant impact on beneficiaries and other stakeholders as well as on the economy in general through its coverage of important health care benefits for the aged and disabled, the payment of premiums and other cost-sharing by those beneficiaries, its payments to providers who supply those health care services, and its interaction with other insurance coverage.

Projections of future Medicare expenditures and funding indicate that the program will place increasing financial demands on the federal budget and on beneficiaries. In response to these concerns, Congress may consider a range of Medicare reform options, from making changes within the current structure, including modifying provider payments and revising existing oversight and regulatory mechanisms, to restructuring the entire program.

The committees of jurisdiction for the mandatory spending (benefits) portion of Medicare are the Senate Committee on Finance, the House Committee on Ways and Means, and the House Committee on Energy and Commerce. The House and Senate Committees on Appropriations have jurisdiction over the discretionary spending used to administer and oversee the program.

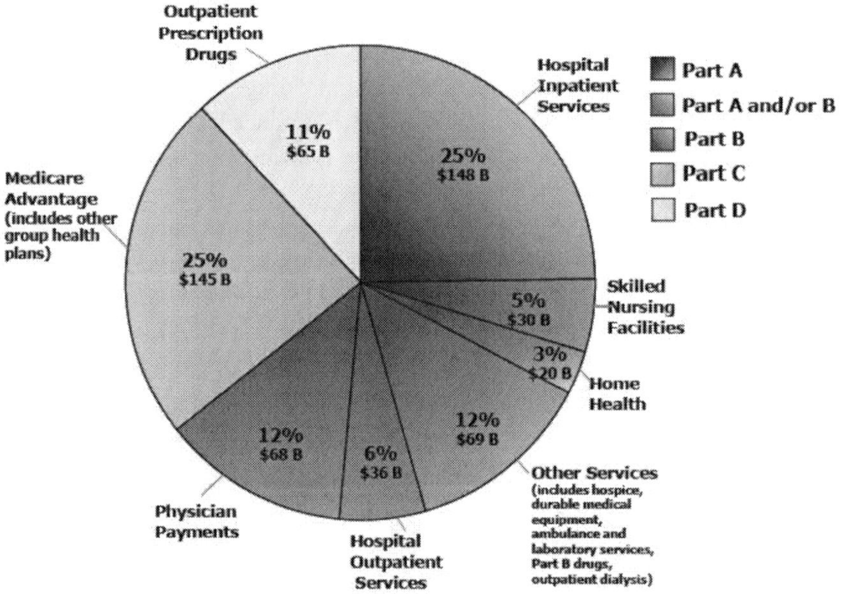

Source: Figure by CRS based on data from the Congressional Budget Office, February 2013 Medicare Baseline.

Notes: *Numbers may not add due to rounding. The $580 billion in benefit payments does not include CBO's estimated reductions under sequestration, administration costs or recoveries.

Figure 1. Projected Medicare Benefit Spending, by Category, FY2013 ($580 Billion*).

MEDICARE HISTORY

Medicare was enacted in 1965 (P.L. 89-97) in response to the concern that only about half of the nation's seniors had health insurance, and most of those had coverage only for inpatient hospital costs. The new program, which became effective July 1, 1966, included Part A coverage for hospital and post-hospital services and Part B coverage for doctors and other medical services. As is the case for the Social Security program, Part A is financed by payroll taxes levied on current workers and their employers; persons must pay into the system for 40 calendar quarters to become entitled to premium-free benefits. Medicare Part B is voluntary, with a monthly premium required of beneficiaries who choose to enroll. Payments to health care providers under both Part A and Part B were originally based on the most common form of payment at the time, namely "reasonable costs" for hospital and other institutional services or "usual, customary and reasonable charges"[3] for physicians and other medical services.

Medicare is considered a social insurance program and is the second largest such federal program, after Social Security. The 1965 law also established Medicaid, the federal/state health insurance program for the poor; this was an expansion of previous welfare-based assistance programs. Some low-income individuals qualify for both Medicare and Medicaid.

In the ensuing years, Medicare has undergone considerable change. P.L. 92-603, enacted in 1972, expanded program coverage to certain individuals under 65 (the disabled and persons with end-stage renal disease (ESRD)),[4] and introduced managed care into Medicare by allowing private insurance entities to provide Medicare benefits in exchange for a monthly capitated payment. This law also began to place limitations on the definitions of reasonable costs and charges in order to gain some control over program spending which, even initially, exceeded original projections.

During the 1980s and 1990s, a number of laws were enacted that included provisions designed to further stem the rapid increase in program spending through modifications to the way payments to providers were determined, and to postpone the insolvency of the Medicare Part A trust fund. This was typically achieved through tightening rules governing payments to providers of services and limiting the annual updates in such payments. The program moved from payments based on reasonable costs and reasonable charges to payment systems under which a predetermined payment amount was established for a specified unit of service. At the same time, beneficiaries were given expanded options to obtain covered services through private managed care arrangements, typically health maintenance organizations (HMOs). Most Medicare payment provisions were incorporated into larger budget reconciliation bills designed to control overall federal spending.

This effort culminated in the enactment of the Balanced Budget Act of 1997 (BBA 97, P.L. 105- 33).[5] This law slowed the rate of growth in payments to providers and established new payment systems for certain categories of providers. It also established the Medicare+Choice program, which expanded private plan options for beneficiaries and changed the way most of these plans were paid. BBA 97 further expanded preventive services covered by the program.

Subsequently, Congress became concerned that the BBA 97 cuts in payments to providers were somewhat larger than originally anticipated. Therefore, legislation was enacted in both 1999 (Balanced Budget Refinement Act of 1999, BBRA, P.L. 106-113) and 2000 (Medicare, Medicaid, and SCHIP Benefits Improvement and Protection Act of 2000, BIPA, P.L. 106-554) to mitigate the impact of BBA 97 on providers.

In 2003, Congress enacted the Medicare Prescription Drug, Improvement, and Modernization Act of 2003 (MMA, P.L. 108-173),[6] which included a major benefit expansion and placed increasing emphasis on the private sector to deliver and manage benefits. The MMA included provisions that (1) created a new voluntary outpatient prescription drug benefit to be administered by private entities; (2) replaced the Medicare+Choice program with the Medicare Advantage (MA) program and raised payments to plans in order to increase their availability for beneficiaries; (3) introduced the concept of income testing into Medicare, with higher-income persons paying larger Part B premiums beginning in 2007;[7] (4) modified some provider payment rules; (5) expanded covered preventive services; and (6) created a specific process for overall program review if general revenue spending exceeded a specified threshold.[8]

During the 109th Congress, two laws were enacted that incorporated minor modifications to Medicare's payment rules. These were the Deficit Reduction Act of 2005 (DRA, P.L. 109-171) and the Tax Relief and Health Care Act of 2006 (TRHCA, P.L. 109-432). In the 110th Congress, additional changes were incorporated in the Medicare, Medicaid, and SCHIP Extension Act of 2007 (MMSEA, P.L. 110-173)[9] and the Medicare Improvements for Patients and Providers Act of 2008 (MIPPA, P.L. 110-275).[10]

In the 111th Congress, comprehensive health reform legislation was enacted that, among other things, made statutory changes to the Medicare program. The Patient Protection and Affordable Care Act (ACA; P.L. 111-148), enacted on March 23, 2010, included numerous provisions affecting

Medicare payments, payment rules, covered benefits, and the delivery of care. The Health Care and Education Affordability Reconciliation Act of 2010 (the Reconciliation Act, or HCERA; P.L. 111-152), enacted on March 30, 2010, made changes to a number of Medicare-related provisions in the ACA and added several new provisions.[11] Included in the ACA, as amended, are provisions that (1) constrain Medicare's annual payment increases for certain providers; (2) change payment rates in the Medicare Advantage program so that they more closely resemble those in fee-for-service; (3) reduce payments to hospitals that serve a large number of low-income patients; (4) create an Independent Payment Advisory Board (IPAB) that will make recommendations to adjust Medicare payment rates;[12] (5) phase out the Part D prescription drug benefit "doughnut hole"; (6) increase resources and enhance activities to prevent fraud and abuse; and (7) provide incentives to increase the quality and efficiency of care, such as creating value-based purchasing programs for certain types of providers, allowing accountable care organizations (ACOs) that meet certain quality and efficiency standards to share in the savings,[13] creating a voluntary pilot program that bundles payments for physician, hospital, and post-acute care services, and adjusting payments to hospitals for readmissions related to certain potentially preventable conditions.

During the first session of the 112th Congress, on August 2, 2011, the Budget Control Act of 2011 (BCA; P.L. 112-25) was enacted. It provided for increases in the debt limit and established procedures designed to reduce the federal budget deficit, including the creation of a Joint Select Committee on Deficit Reduction.[14] The failure of the Joint Committee to propose budget reduction legislation by its mandated deadline triggered automatic spending reductions ("sequestration") in years 2013 through 2021. The American Taxpayer Relief Act of 2012 (ATRA, P.L. 112-240), signed into law January 2, 2013, delayed the automatic reductions by two months.[15] Unless Congress takes action to prevent these cuts, most Medicare program expenditures will be subject to reductions of up to 2% each year.[16]

Under sequestration, Medicare's benefit structure would generally remain unchanged; however, most Medicare plans and providers would see a reduction in their Medicare payments. Spending for certain Medicare payments is exempt from sequestration and would therefore not be reduced. These exemptions include (1) Part D low-income subsidies, (2) the Part D catastrophic subsidy, and (3) Qualified Individual (QI) premiums. Some Medicare administrative and operational expenditures could be subject to reductions higher than 2%.[17] Prior to the enactment of ATRA, CBO estimated that Medicare spending reductions would total approximately $123 billion over nine years.[18]

Eligibility and Enrollment

Most persons aged 65 or older are automatically entitled to premium-free Part A because they or their spouse paid Medicare payroll taxes for at least 40 quarters (10 years) on earnings covered by either the Social Security or the Railroad Retirement systems. Persons under age 65 who receive cash disability benefits from Social Security or the Railroad Retirement systems for at least 24 months are also entitled to Part A. (Since there is a five-month waiting period for cash payments, the Medicare waiting period is effectively 29 months.)[19] The 24-month waiting period is waived for persons with amyotrophic lateral sclerosis (ALS, "Lou Gehrig's disease"). Individuals of any age with ESRD who receive dialysis on a regular basis or a kidney transplant are eligible for Medicare. Medicare coverage for individuals with ESRD usually starts the first day of the fourth month of dialysis treatments. In addition, individuals with one or more specified lung diseases or types of cancer who lived for six months during a specified period prior to diagnosis in an area subject to a public health emergency declaration by the Environmental Protection Agency (EPA) as of June 17, 2009, are also deemed entitled to benefits under Part A and eligible to enroll in Part B.

Persons over age 65 who are not entitled to premium-free Part A may obtain coverage by paying a monthly premium ($441 in 2013) or, for persons with at least 30 quarters of covered employment, a reduced monthly premium ($243 in 2013). In addition, disabled persons who lose their cash benefits solely because of higher earnings, and subsequently lose their extended Medicare coverage, may continue their Medicare enrollment by paying a premium, subject to limitations.

Generally, enrollment in Medicare Part B is voluntary. All persons entitled to Part A (and persons over 65 not entitled to premium-free Part A) may enroll in Part B by paying a monthly premium.[20] For most Part B enrollees, the 2013 monthly premium is $104.90. Higher income enrollees pay higher premiums. (See the "Part B Financing" section below.) While enrollment in Part B is voluntary for most individuals, in most cases, those who voluntarily enroll in Part A must also enroll in Part B. Additionally, ESRD beneficiaries and Medicare Advantage enrollees (discussed below) must also enroll in Part B.

Together, Parts A and B of Medicare comprise "original Medicare," which covers benefits on a fee-for-service (FFS) basis. Beneficiaries have another option for coverage through private plans, called the Medicare Advantage (MA or Part C) program. When beneficiaries first become eligible for Medicare, they may choose either original Medicare or they may enroll in a private MA plan. Each fall, there is an annual open enrollment period during which time Medicare beneficiaries may choose a different MA plan, or leave or join the MA program.[21] Beneficiaries are to receive information about their options to help them make informed decisions.[22] In 2013, the annual open enrollment period will be from October 15 to December 7 for plan choices starting the following January. Starting in 2012, MA plans with a 5-star quality rating are allowed to enroll Medicare beneficiaries who are either in traditional Medicare or in an MA plan with a lower quality rating at any time.

Finally, each individual enrolled in either Part A or Part B is also entitled to obtain qualified prescription drug coverage through enrollment in a Part D prescription drug plan. Similar to Part B, enrollment in Part D is voluntary and the beneficiary pays a monthly premium. Beginning in 2011, some higher-income enrollees pay higher premiums, similar to enrollees in Part B. Generally, beneficiaries enrolled in an MA plan providing qualified prescription drug coverage (MA-PD plan) must obtain their prescription drug coverage through that plan.[23]

In general, individuals who do not enroll in Part B or Part D during an initial enrollment period (when they first become eligible for Medicare) must pay a permanent penalty of increased monthly premiums if they choose to enroll at a later date. Individuals who do not enroll in Part B during their initial enrollment period may enroll only during the annual open enrollment period, which occurs from January 1 to March 31 each year. Coverage begins the following July 1. However, the law waives the Part B late enrollment penalty for current workers who have primary coverage through their own or a spouse's employer-sponsored plan. These individuals have a special enrollment period once their employment ends; as long as they enroll in Part B during this time, they will not be subject to penalty.[24]

Individuals who do not enroll in Part D during their initial enrollment period may enroll during the annual open enrollment period, which corresponds with the Part C annual enrollment period—from October 15 to December 7, with coverage effective the following January. Individuals are not subject to the Part D penalty if they have maintained "creditable" drug coverage through another source, such as retiree health coverage offered by a former employer or union. However, once employees retire or have no access to "creditable" Part D coverage, a penalty will apply unless they sign up for coverage during a special enrollment period. Finally, for persons who qualify for the low-income subsidy for Part D, the delayed-enrollment penalty does not apply.

BENEFITS AND PAYMENTS

Medicare Parts A, B, and D each cover different services, with Part C providing a private plan alternative for Medicare services, except hospice. The Parts A-D covered services are described below, along with a description of Medicare's payments.

Part A

Part A provides coverage for inpatient hospital services, post-hospital skilled nursing facility (SNF) services, hospice care, and some home health services, subject to certain conditions and limitations. Approximately 18% of Part A enrollees use Part A services during a year.

Inpatient Hospital Services

Medicare inpatient hospital services include (1) bed and board; (2) nursing services; (3) use of hospital facilities; (4) drugs, biologics, supplies, appliances, and equipment; and (5) diagnostic and therapeutic items and services. (Physicians' services provided during an inpatient stay are paid under the physician fee schedule and discussed below in the "Physicians and Non-physician Practitioner Services" section.) Coverage for inpatient services is linked to an individual's benefit period or "spell of illness" (defined as beginning on the day a patient enters a hospital and ending when he or she has not been in a hospital or skilled nursing facility for 60 days). An individual admitted to a hospital more than 60 days after the last discharge from a hospital or SNF begins a new benefit period. Coverage in each benefit period is subject to the following conditions:

- Days 1-60. Beneficiary pays a deductible ($1,184 in 2013).
- Days 61-90. Beneficiary pays a *daily* coinsurance charge ($296 in 2013).

- Days 91-150. After 90 days, the beneficiary may draw on one or more of 60 lifetime reserve days, provided they have not been previously used. (Each of the 60 lifetime reserve days can be used only once during an individual's lifetime.) For lifetime reserve days, the beneficiary pays a daily coinsurance charge ($592 in 2013); otherwise the beneficiary pays all costs.
- Days 151 and over. Beneficiary pays for all costs for these days.

Inpatient mental health care in a psychiatric facility is limited to 190 days during a patient's lifetime. Cost sharing is structured similarly to that for stays in a general hospital (above).

Medicare makes payments to most acute care hospitals under the inpatient prospective payment (IPPS) system, using a prospectively determined amount for each discharge. Medicare's payments to hospitals is the product of two components: (1) a discharge payment amount adjusted by a wage index for the area where the hospital is located or where it has been reclassified, and (2) the weight associated with the Medicare severity-diagnosis related group (MS-DRG) to which the patient is assigned. This weight reflects the relative costliness of the average patient in that MS-DRG, which is revised annually, generally effective October 1st of each year.

Additional payments are made to hospitals for cases with extraordinary costs (outliers), indirect costs incurred by teaching hospitals for graduate medical education, and disproportionate share hospital (DSH) payments to those hospitals serving a certain volume of low-income patients. Additional payments may also be made for qualified new technologies that have been approved for special add-on payments. In FY2013, certain low volume hospitals will receive an add-on payment for each Medicare discharge, an amount that ranges from 25% for hospitals with less than 200 Medicare discharges to no adjustment for hospitals with more than 1,600 Medicare discharges. Prospective payments are also made for inpatient capital costs.

Medicare also makes payments outside the IPPS system for direct costs associated with graduate medical education (GME) for hospital residents, subject to certain limits. In addition, Medicare reimburses hospitals for 65% of the allowable costs associated with beneficiaries' unpaid deductible and copayment amounts as well as for the costs for certain other services.

Additional payments or special treatment may apply for hospitals meeting one of the following designations: (1) sole community hospitals (SCHs), (2) Medicare dependent hospitals, and (3) rural referral centers. Certain hospitals or distinct hospital units are exempt from IPPS and paid on an alternative basis,[25] including (1) inpatient rehabilitation facilities, (2) long-term care hospitals, (3) psychiatric facilities including hospitals and distinct part units, (4) children's hospitals and cancer hospitals, and (5) critical access hospitals.

Skilled Nursing Facility (SNF) Services

Medicare covers up to 100 days of post-hospital care for persons needing skilled nursing or rehabilitation services on a daily basis.[26] The SNF stay must be preceded by an inpatient hospital stay of at least three days, and the transfer to the SNF typically must occur within 30 days of the hospital discharge. There is no beneficiary cost-sharing for the first 20 days of a Medicare-covered SNF stay. For days 21 to 100 beneficiaries are subject to daily coinsurance charges ($148 in 2013). The 100-day limit begins again with a new spell of illness.

SNF services are paid under a prospective payment system (PPS), which is based on a per diem urban or rural base payment rate, adjusted for case mix (average severity of illness) and area wages. The per diem rate generally covers all services, including room and board, provided to the patient that day. The case-mix adjustment is made using the resource utilization groups (RUGs) classification system, which uses patient assessments to assign a beneficiary to one of 66 groups that reflect the beneficiary's expected use of services. Patient assessments are done at various times during a patient's stay and the RUG category a beneficiary is placed in can change with changes in the beneficiary's condition. Extra payments are not made for extraordinarily costly cases ("outliers").

Hospice Care

The Medicare hospice benefit covers services designed to provide palliative care and management of a terminal illness; the benefit includes drugs and medical and support services. These services are provided to Medicare beneficiaries with a life expectancy of six months or less for two 90-day periods, followed by an unlimited number of 60-day periods. The individual's attending physician and the hospice physician must certify the need for the first benefit period, but only the hospice physician needs to recertify for subsequent periods. Starting January 1, 2011, a hospice physician or nurse practitioner must have a face-to-face encounter with the individual to determine continued eligibility prior to the 180th day recertification, and for each subsequent recertification. Hospice care is provided in lieu of most other Medicare services related to the curative treatment of the terminal illness. Beneficiaries electing hospice care from a hospice program may receive curative services for illnesses or injuries unrelated to their terminal illness and they may disenroll from the hospice at any time. Nominal cost-sharing is required for drugs and respite care.

Payment for hospice care is based on one of four prospectively determined rates (which correspond to four different levels of care) for each day a beneficiary is under the care of the hospice. The four rate categories are routine home care, continuous home care, inpatient respite care, and general inpatient care. Payment rates are adjusted to reflect differences in area wage levels, using the hospital wage index.[27] Payments to a hospice are subject to an aggregate cap based on a cap amount and the number of beneficiaries who received hospice services during the cap year (November 1 to October 31). The cap amount is adjusted annually by changes to the medical care expenditure category of the Consumer Price Index for all urban consumers (CPI-U).

Parts A and B

Home health services and services for individuals with end-stage renal disease are covered under both Parts A and B of Medicare.

Home Health Services

Medicare covers visits by participating home health agencies for beneficiaries who (1) are confined to home, (2) need skilled nursing care on an intermittent basis, or (3) need physical or occupational therapy or speech language therapy. After establishing such eligibility, the continuing need for occupational therapy services may extend the eligibility period. Covered services include part-time or intermittent nursing care, physical or occupational therapy or speech language pathology services, medical social services, home health aide services, and medical supplies and durable medical equipment. The services must be provided under a plan of care established by a physician, and the plan must be reviewed by the physician at least every 60 days.

Home health services are covered under both Medicare Parts A and B. Part A covers up to 100 visits following a stay in a hospital or SNF. Part A also covers all home health services for persons not enrolled in Part B. All other home health services are covered under Part B. There is no beneficiary cost-sharing for home health services (though some other Part B services provided in connection with the visit, such as durable medical equipment, are subject to cost-sharing charges).

Home health services are paid under a home health PPS, based on 60-day episodes of care; a patient may have an unlimited number of episodes. Under the PPS, for episodes with five or greater visits a nationwide base payment amount is adjusted by differences in wages (using the hospital wage index). This amount is then adjusted for case mix using the applicable Home Health Resource Group (HHRG) to which the beneficiary has been assigned. The HHRG applicable to a beneficiary is determined following an assessment of the patient's condition and care needs using the Outcome and Assessment Information Set (OASIS); there are 153 HHRGs. For episodes with four or fewer visits, the PPS reimburses the provider for each visit performed. Further payment adjustments may be made for services provided in rural areas, outlier visits (for extremely costly patients), a partial episode for beneficiaries that have an intervening event during their episode, or an agency's failure to submit quality data to CMS.

End-Stage Renal Disease (ESRD)

Individuals with ESRD are eligible for all services covered under Parts A and B. Kidney transplantation services, to the extent they are inpatient hospital services, are subject to the inpatient hospital PPS and are reimbursed by both Parts A and B. However, kidney acquisition costs are paid on a reasonable cost basis under Part A. Dialysis treatments, when an individual is admitted to a hospital, are covered under Part A.

Individuals with ESRD are eligible for all Part B Services. Part B also covers their dialysis services, drugs, biologicals (including erythropoiesis stimulating agents used in treating anemia as a result of ESRD), diagnostic laboratory tests, and other items and services furnished to individuals for the treatment of ESRD.

In effect since January 1, 2011, the new ESRD prospective payment system (PPS) makes no payment distinction as to the site where renal dialysis services are provided. With the implementation of the ESRD PPS, Medicare dialysis payments are bundled (phased in over four years, 2011 through 2014) using a single payment for Medicare renal dialysis services that includes (1) items and services included in the former payment system's base rate as of December 31, 2010; (2) erythropoiesis stimulating agents (ESAs) for the treatment of ESRD; (3) other drugs and biologicals for which payment was made separately (before bundling); and (4) diagnostic laboratory tests and other items and services furnished to individuals for the treatment of ESRD.

The new system is case-mix adjusted based on factors such as patient weight, body mass index, comorbidities, length of time on dialysis, age, race, ethnicity, and other appropriate factors as determined by the Secretary of Health and Human Services. Under the ESRD Quality Incentive Program, dialysis facilities that fail to meet the performance standards of the ESRD-related quality measures receive reduced payments.

Part B

Medicare Part B covers physicians' services, outpatient hospital services, durable medical equipment, and other medical services. Initially, over 98% of the eligible population voluntarily enrolled in Part B, but in recent years, the percentage has fallen to about 93%.[28] Over 70% of Part B enrollees use Part B services during a year. The program generally pays 80% of the approved amount (most commonly, a fee schedule or other predetermined amount) for covered services in excess of the annual deductible ($147 in 2013). The beneficiary is liable for the remaining 20%.

Most providers and practitioners are subject to limits on amounts they can bill beneficiaries for covered services. For example, physicians and some other practitioners may choose whether or not to accept "assignment" on a claim. When a physician accepts assignment, the physician can only bill the beneficiary the 20% coinsurance plus any unmet deductible. When a physician agrees to accept assignment on all Medicare claims in a given year, the physician is referred to as a "participating physician." There are several advantages to being a participating provider, including higher reimbursement under the Medicare fee schedule, a lower beneficiary copayment, and automatic forwarding of Medigap claims.

Physicians who do not agree to accept assignment on all Medicare claims in a given year are referred to as nonparticipating physicians. Nonparticipating physicians may or may not accept assignment for a given service. If they do not, they may charge beneficiaries more than the fee schedule amount on nonassigned claims; however, these "balance billing" charges are subject to certain limits. Alternatively, physicians may choose not to accept any Medicare payment and enter into private contracts with their patients.

For some providers, such as nurse practitioners and physician assistants, assignment is mandatory; these providers can only bill the beneficiary the 20% coinsurance and any unmet deductible. For other Part B services, such as durable medical equipment, assignment is optional; for these services, applicable providers may bill beneficiaries for amounts above Medicare's recognized payment level and may do so without limit.[29]

Physicians and Non-physician Practitioner Services

Medicare Part B covers medically necessary doctors' services and medical services provided by some non-physician practitioners. Certain limitations apply for services provided by chiropractors and podiatrists. Beneficiary cost-sharing is typically 20% of the approved amount, although preventive care services require no coinsurance from the beneficiary and outpatient mental health services are currently in the fourth of a five-year phase-in that will reduce beneficiary responsibility from 50% to 20% by 2014.[30] Covered non-physician practitioner services include, but are not limited to, those provided by physician assistants, nurse practitioners, certified registered nurse anesthetists, and clinical social workers.

A number of Part B services are paid under the physician fee schedule. These include services of physicians, non-physician practitioners, and therapists. Most services described below are paid under the physician fee schedule. There are over 7,000 service codes under the fee schedule.

The fee schedule assigns relative values to each service code. These relative values reflect physician work (based on time, skill, and intensity involved), practice expenses, and malpractice expenses. The relative values are adjusted for geographic variations in the costs of practicing medicine. These geographically adjusted relative values are converted into a dollar payment amount by a national conversion factor. The conversion factor is updated each year by a formula specified in law. The update percentage is based on the Medicare Economic Index (MEI, which measures changes in the prices of the inputs required to provide physician services) subject to an adjustment to match spending under the sustainable growth rate (SGR) system, which establishes a target for total cumulative expenditures since 1996.[31] If total expenditures exceed the target, the update for a future year is reduced. Application of the SGR formula would have led to negative updates each year since 2002. However, Congress has acted several times to avert reductions, thereby overriding the statutory formula for the 2003-2013 period. In recent years, the update to the conversion factor was 0% (compared to 2009 payment levels) for January through May 2010 and 2.2% for June 2010 through December 2012.[32] The ATRA extends the SGR override for another year and maintains physician fee schedule payments at the 2012 level through December 2013.[33]

In addition to the fee schedule reimbursements, physicians who report on selected quality measures for services for which quality measures are established will receive bonus payments for those services provided beginning in July 2007. The bonus payments were 1.5% during the second half of 2007 and for 2008, 2.0% for 2009 and 2010, 1.0% for 2011, and 0.5% in 2012. The bonus remains at 0.5% in 2013 and 2014 for those who successfully report the measures. Subsequently, those providers who fail to successfully report the measures will be subject to a 1.5% penalty in 2015 and a 2% penalty in 2016 and future years. Additional bonus payments will be made for 2009-2013 for Medicare professionals providing covered services who are successful electronic prescribers and in 2011-2014 for those who meet the requirements of a Maintenance of Certification Program (MOCP).[34]

Therapy Services

Medicare covers medically necessary outpatient physician and occupational therapy, and speech-language pathology services. The program has limits (therapy caps) on how much it pays for outpatient therapy services in a calendar year. These limits are updated annually. In 2013, the annual therapy cap amounts are (1) $1,900 for outpatient physical therapy services and speech language pathology services; and (2) $1,900 for outpatient occupational therapy services. The limits apply to services provided in the following settings: physical therapists in private practice, physician offices, skilled nursing facilities (when not covered under Part A), comprehensive outpatient rehabilitation facilities (CORFs) and other rehabilitation agencies, critical access hospitals (CAHs), and hospital outpatient departments.[35]

The DRA required the Secretary to implement an exceptions process to allow continued coverage for medically necessary services after a beneficiary has reached the therapy cap, up to a certain limit. A series of legislative acts have extended the exceptions process and increased the limits each year since then. In 2013, Medicare will continue to pay for therapy costs above the $1,900 cap up to $3,700 for each category of therapy service for beneficiaries who qualify for the exception. Under certain conditions, Medicare may pay for therapy costs that exceed $3,700 a year; however, claims for such services require supporting documentation from the therapy provider and are subject to a higher level of review by Medicare.

Preventive Services

The original Medicare statute prohibited payment for covered items and services that are "not reasonable and necessary for the diagnosis or treatment of illness or injury or to improve the functioning of a malformed body member," which effectively excluded preventive and screening services.[36] In recent years, Congress has added and expanded Medicare coverage for a number of such services through legislation, including MMA, MIPPA, and ACA. Under current law, if a preventive service is recommended for use by the U.S. Preventive Services Task Force (USPSTF, an independent evidence-review panel)[37] and Medicare covers the service, all cost-sharing must be waived. Also, the HHS Secretary may add coverage of a USPSTF-recommended service that is not already covered. Coverage for preventive and screening services currently includes, among other services: (1) a "welcome to Medicare" physical exam during the first year of enrollment in Part B and an annual visit and prevention plan thereafter; (2) flu vaccine (annual), pneumococcal vaccine, and hepatitis B vaccine (for persons at high risk); (3) screening tests for breast, cervical, prostate, and colorectal cancers; (4) screening for other conditions such as depression, heart disease, glaucoma, and osteoporosis; and (5) intensive behavioral therapy for heart disease and for obesity.[38] These services are covered under the Medicare Part B fee schedule.

Clinical Laboratory and other Diagnostic Tests

Part B covers outpatient clinical laboratory tests, such as certain blood tests, urinalysis, and some screening tests, provided by Medicare-participating laboratories. These services may be furnished by labs located in hospitals and physician offices, as well as by independent labs. Beneficiaries have no copayments or deductibles for covered clinical lab services.

Payment for outpatient clinical laboratory services are made on the basis of the clinical laboratory fee schedule (CLFS) and are the lesser of the amount billed, the local fee for a geographic area, or a national limit; the national limits are set at a percentage (74%) of the median of all local fee schedule amounts for each laboratory test code. In general, annual increases in clinical lab fees are based on the percentage change in the CPI-U. However, Congress has modified the update in recent years by (1) freezing the fee schedule amounts through 2008, (2) reducing the update that would otherwise apply by 0.5 percentage points for 2009-2010, (3) establishing a permanent multi-factor productivity adjustment and a 1.75 percentage point reduction for years 2011 through 2015, and (4) requiring an additional -2.0 percent rebasing of the CLFS. As a result of these actions, the annual update to the local clinical laboratory fee schedule for CY2013 decreases payment by 2.95%.[39]

Part B also covers diagnostic x-ray tests and other diagnostic tests, as well as x-ray, radium, and radioisotope therapy. Generally, these services are paid for under the physician fee schedule.

Durable Medical Equipment, Prosthetics, Orthotics and Supplies (DMEPOS)

Medicare covers a wide variety of equipment and devices under the heading of durable medical equipment (DME), and prosthetics, orthotics (PO) if they are medically necessary and are prescribed by a physician. DME is defined as equipment that (1) can withstand repeated use, (2) is used primarily to serve a medical purpose, (3) is not generally useful in the absence of an illness or injury, and (4) is appropriate for use in the home. DME includes such items as hospital beds, wheelchairs, blood glucose monitors, and oxygen and oxygen equipment. It also includes related supplies, such as drugs and biologics that are necessary for the effective use of the product. PO is defined as items that replace all or part of a body organ, such as colostomy bags and pacemakers, as well as leg, arm, back, and neck braces and artificial legs, arms, and eyes. Medicare also covers some items or supplies (S), such as disposable surgical dressings that do not meet the definitions of DME or PO.

Except in competitive bidding areas (described below), Medicare pays for most DMEPOS based on fee schedules. Medicare pays 80% of the lower of the supplier's charge for the item or the fee schedule amount. The beneficiary is responsible for the remaining 20%. In general, fee schedule amounts are updated each year by a (1) measure of price inflation, and (2) a measure of economy-wide productivity, which may result in lower fee schedule amounts from one year to the nest.

Numerous studies and investigations have shown that Medicare pays more for certain items of DME and PO than some other health insurers and some retail outlets.[40] Such overpayments may be due partly to the fee schedule mechanism of payment. MMA required the Secretary to establish a Competitive Acquisition Program for certain DMEPOS in specified areas. Instead of paying for medical equipment based on a fee schedule established by law, payment for items in competitive bidding areas is based on the supplier bids. MIPPA delayed the program and required the first round of the program to be re-bid, in addition to other changes. The re-bid took place in 2009 and the program started in nine metropolitan areas in January 2011.[41] The second round will expand the program to 91 additional areas. Bidding for round 2 began in January 2012, with payments based on those bids starting in July 2013.

Part B Drugs and Biologics[42]

Certain specified outpatient prescription drugs and biologics are covered under Medicare Part B. (However, most outpatient prescription drugs are covered under Part D, discussed below.) Covered Part B drugs and biologics include drugs furnished incident to physicians' services, immunosuppressive drugs following a Medicare-covered organ transplant, erythropoietin for treatment of anemia for persons with ESRD, oral anti-cancer drugs (provided they have the same active ingredients and are used for the same indications as chemotherapy drugs which would be covered if furnished incident to physicians services), and drugs needed for the effective use of DME. Generally, Medicare's reimbursement for Part B covered drugs equals 106% of the drug manufacturer's reported average sales price (ASP). Health care providers also receive a separate payment for administering Medicare Part B drugs. Medicare pays 80% of the amount paid to providers, while the beneficiaries are responsible for the remaining 20%.

Hospital Outpatient Department Services

Hospitals provide two distinct types of services to outpatients: services that are diagnostic in nature, and other services that aid the physician in the treatment of the patient. A hospital outpatient is a person who has not been admitted by the hospital as an inpatient but is registered on the hospital records as an outpatient. Generally, payments under the hospital outpatient prospective payment system (OPPS) cover the operating and capital-related costs that are directly related and integral to performing a procedure or furnishing a service on an outpatient basis. These payments cover services such as the use of an operating suite, treatment, procedure or recovery room; use of an observation bed as well as anesthesia; certain drugs or pharmaceuticals; incidental services; and other necessary or implantable supplies or services. Payments for services such as those provided by physicians and other professionals as well as therapy and clinical diagnostic laboratory services, among others, are separate.

Under the OPPS, the unit of payment for acute care hospitals is the individual service or procedure as assigned to an ambulatory payment classification (APC). To the extent possible, integral services and items (excluding physician services paid under the physician fee schedule) are bundled within each APC. Specified new technologies are assigned to "new technology APCs" until clinical and cost data are available to permit assignment into a "clinical APC." Medicare's hospital outpatient payment is calculated by multiplying the relative weight associated with an APC by a conversion factor. For most APCs, 60% of the conversion factor is geographically adjusted by the wage index used for the inpatient prospective payment system. Except for new technology APCs, each APC has a relative weight that is based on the median cost of services in that APC. The OPPS also includes pass-through payments for new technologies (specific drugs, biologicals, and devices) and payments for outliers.[43]

Ambulatory Surgical Center Services

An ambulatory surgical center (ASC) is a distinct entity that furnishes outpatient surgical procedures to patients who do not require an overnight stay after the procedure. According to MedPAC, most ASCs are freestanding facilities rather than part of a larger facility, such as a hospital. Medicare covers surgical and medical services performed in an ambulatory surgical center (ASC) that are (1) commonly performed on an inpatient basis but may be safely performed in an ASC; (2) not of a type that are commonly performed or that may be safely performed in physicians' offices; (3) limited to procedures requiring a dedicated operating room or suite and generally requiring a post-operative recovery room or short term (not overnight) convalescent room; and (4) not otherwise excluded from Medicare coverage.

Beginning in January 2008, Medicare pays for surgery-related facility services provided in ASCs using a payment system based on the OPPS. (Associated physician fees are paid for separately under the physician fee schedule.) Each of the 3,300 procedures approved for payment in an ASC is classified into an ambulatory payment classification (APC) group on the basis of clinical and cost similarity. The ASC system uses the same payment groups (APCs) as the OPPS, and for most procedures, the same relative weights used in the OPPS also apply. The ASC system uses a conversion factor based on a percentage of the OPPS conversion factor. The percentage of this average dollar figure is set to ensure budget neutrality, so that total payments under the new ASC payment system should equal total payments under the old ASC payment system. A different payment method is used to set ASC payment for new, office-based procedures, separately payable drugs, and device-intensive procedures.[44] This policy also applies to separately payable radiology services. Separately payable drugs in an ASC are paid the same amount as if provided in a hospital outpatient department. Different rules apply for device intensive procedures (where a device that is packaged into an APC accounts for more than half of its total payments). Separate payments are made for corneal tissue acquisition, brachytherapy sources, certain radiology services, many drugs, and certain implantable devices.

Ambulance

Medicare Part B covers emergency and non-emergency ambulance services to or from a hospital, critical access hospital (CAH), or a skilled nursing facility (SNF) when other modes of transportation could endanger the Medicare beneficiary's health. In most cases, the program covers 80% of the allowed amount for the service, and the beneficiary is responsible for the remaining 20%. Generally, ambulance services are covered if (1) transportation of the beneficiary occurs; (2) the beneficiary is taken to an appropriate location (generally, the closest appropriate facility); (3) the ambulance service is medically necessary (other forms of transportation are contraindicated); (4) the ambulance provider or supplier meets state licensing requirements; and (5) the transportation is not part of a Medicare Part A covered stay.[45] Medicare covers both scheduled and nonscheduled nonemergency transports if the beneficiary is bed-confined or meets other medical necessity criteria. Medicare may also cover emergency ambulance transportation in an airplane or helicopter if the beneficiary's location is not easily reached by ground transportation or if long distance or obstacles, such as heavy traffic, would prevent the individual from obtaining needed care.

Medicare pays for different levels of ambulance services, which reflect the staff training and equipment required to meet the patient's medical condition or health needs. Generally, basic life support (BLS) is provided by emergency medical technicians (EMTs). Advanced life support (ALS) is provided by EMTs with advanced training or by paramedics. Medicare pays for ambulance services according to a national fee schedule. The fee schedule establishes seven categories of ground ambulance services and two categories of air ambulance services. Some rural ground and air ambulance services may qualify for increased payments.[46] Ambulance providers that are CAHs, or that are entities that are owned and operated by a CAH, are paid on a reasonable cost basis if they are the only ambulance provider within a 35 mile radius.

Rural Health Clinics and Federally Qualified Health Centers

Medicare covers Part B services in rural health clinics (RHCs) and federally qualified health centers (FQHCs) provided by (1) physicians and specified non-physician practitioners; (2) visiting nurses for homebound patients in home health shortage areas; (3) registered dieticians or nutritional professionals for diabetes training and medical nutrition therapy; and (4) others, as well as otherwise covered drugs.

RHCs and FQHCs are paid based on an "all-inclusive" rate per beneficiary visit subject to a per visit upper limit, adjusted annually for inflation.

Part C, Medicare Advantage

Medicare Advantage (MA) is an alternative way for Medicare beneficiaries to receive covered benefits. Under MA, private health plans are paid a per-person amount to provide all Medicare covered benefits (except hospice) to beneficiaries who enroll in their plan. Medicare beneficiaries who are eligible for Part A, enrolled in Part B, and do not have ESRD are eligible to enroll in an MA plan if one is available in their area. Some MA plans may choose their service area (local MA plans), while others agree to serve one or more regions defined by the Secretary (regional MA plans). As of December 2012, nearly all Medicare beneficiaries had access to an MA plan and approximately 27% of beneficiaries were enrolled in one. Private plans may use different techniques to influence the medical care used by enrollees. Some plans, such as health maintenance organizations (HMOs), may require enrollees to receive care from a restricted network of medical providers; enrollees may be required to see a primary care physician who will coordinate their care and refer them to specialists as necessary. Other types of private plans, such as private fee-for-service (PFFS) plans, may look more like original Medicare, with fewer restrictions on the providers an enrollee can see and minimal coordination of care.

In general, MA plans offer additional benefits or require smaller co-payments or deductibles than original Medicare. Sometimes beneficiaries pay for these additional benefits through a higher monthly premium, but sometimes they are financed through plan savings. The extent of extra benefits and reduced cost-sharing varies by plan type and geography. However, Medicare Advantage plans are seen by some beneficiaries as an attractive alternative to more expensive supplemental insurance policies found in the private market.

By contract with CMS, a plan agrees to provide all required services covered in return for a capitated monthly payment adjusted for the demographics and health history of actually enrolled beneficiaries. The same monthly payment is made regardless of how many or few services a beneficiary actually uses. The plan is at-risk if costs, in the aggregate, exceed program payments; conversely, the plan can retain savings if aggregate costs are less than payments. Payments to MA plans are based on a comparison of each plan's estimated cost of providing Medicare covered services (a bid) relative to the maximum amount the federal government will pay for providing those services in the plan's service area (a benchmark). If a plan's bid is less than the benchmark, its payment equals its bid plus a rebate. Starting in 2012, the size of the rebate will be dependent on plan quality and will range from 50% to 70% of the difference between the bid and the benchmark. The rebate must be returned to enrollees in the form of either additional benefits, reduced cost-sharing, reduced Part B or Part D premiums, or some combination of these options. If a plan's bid is equal to or above the benchmark, its payment will be the benchmark amount and each enrollee in that plan will pay an additional premium, equal to the amount by which the bid exceeds the benchmark.

The MA benchmarks are determined through statutorily specified formulas that have changed over time. Since BBA 97, formulas have increased the benchmark amounts, in part, to encourage plan participation in all areas of the country. As a result, however, the benchmark amounts (and plan payments) in some areas are higher than the average cost of original FFS Medicare. The ACA changed the way benchmarks are calculated by tying them closer to (or below) spending in FFS Medicare, and adjusting them based on plan quality. At the time of passage, the Congressional Budget Office expected the ACA changes to result in reduced MA enrollment and plan subsidies for extra benefits, though the impact was expected to vary by market.

Subsequently, the Secretary announced an MA plan quality demonstration to test whether different structures of bonus payments lead to greater quality improvements. The demonstration increases the size of the quality-adjusted benchmarks above levels authorized in the ACA, and expands the number of plans eligible to receive quality-adjusted benchmarks. The demonstration may mitigate some of the reductions in enrollment and extra plan benefits that had been expected with the passage of the ACA.

In 2006, the MA program began to offer MA regional plans. Regional MA plans must agree to serve one or more regions designated by the Secretary. There are 26 MA regions consisting of states or groups of states. Regional plan benchmarks include two components: (1) a statutorily determined amount (comparable to benchmarks described above) and (2) a weighted average of plan bids. Thus, a portion of the benchmark is competitively determined. Similar to local plans, plans with bids below the benchmark are given a rebate, while plans with bids above the benchmark require an additional enrollee premium.

In general, MA eligible individuals may enroll in any MA plan that serves their area. However, some MA plans may restrict their enrollment to beneficiaries who meet additional criteria. For example, employer-sponsored MA plans are generally only available to the retirees of the company sponsoring the plan. In addition, Medicare Special Needs Plans (SNPs) are a type of coordinated care MA plan that exclusively enrolls, or enrolls a disproportionate percentage of, special needs individuals. Special needs individuals are any MA eligible individuals who are either institutionalized as defined by the Secretary, eligible for both Medicare and Medicaid, or have a severe or disabling chronic condition and would benefit from enrollment in a specialized MA plan.

Part D

Medicare Part D provides coverage of outpatient prescription drugs to Medicare beneficiaries who choose to enroll in this optional benefit.[47] (As previously discussed, Part B provides limited coverage of some outpatient prescription drugs.) In 2012, about 60% of eligible Medicare beneficiaries enrolled in Part D. Prescription drug coverage is provided through private prescription drug plans (PDPs), which offer only prescription drug coverage, or through Medicare Advantage prescription drug plans (MA-PDs), which offer prescription drug coverage that is integrated with the health care coverage they provide to Medicare beneficiaries under Part C. Plans must meet certain minimum requirements; however, there are significant variations among them in benefit design, including differences in premiums, drugs included on plan formularies, and cost-sharing for particular drugs.

Qualified Part D prescription drug plans are required to offer either "standard coverage" or alternative coverage that has actuarially equivalent benefits. In 2013, "standard coverage" has a $325 deductible and a 25% coinsurance for costs between $325 and $2,970. From this point, there is minimal coverage until the beneficiary has out-of-pocket costs of $4,750 (about $6,733.75 in total spending); this coverage gap has been labeled the "doughnut hole."[48] Once the beneficiary reaches the catastrophic limit, the program pays all costs except for nominal cost-sharing. In 2010, Medicare sent a tax free, one-time $250 rebate check to each Part D enrollee who reached the doughnut hole. Starting in 2011, the coverage gap is being gradually reduced each year until it is eliminated in 2020.[49] In 2013, a 50% discount is provided by drug manufacturers and Medicare pays an additional 2.5% of the cost of brand-name drugs dispensed during the coverage gap. In 2013, Medicare also pays 21% of the cost of generic drugs dispensed during the coverage gap. (See Figure 2.) By 2020, through a combination of manufacturer discounts and increased Medicare coverage, Part D enrollees will be responsible for 25% of the costs in the coverage gap (the same as during the initial coverage period).

Most plans offer actuarially equivalent benefits rather than the standard package, including alternatives such as reducing or eliminating the deductible, or using tiered cost-sharing with lower cost-sharing for generic drugs.

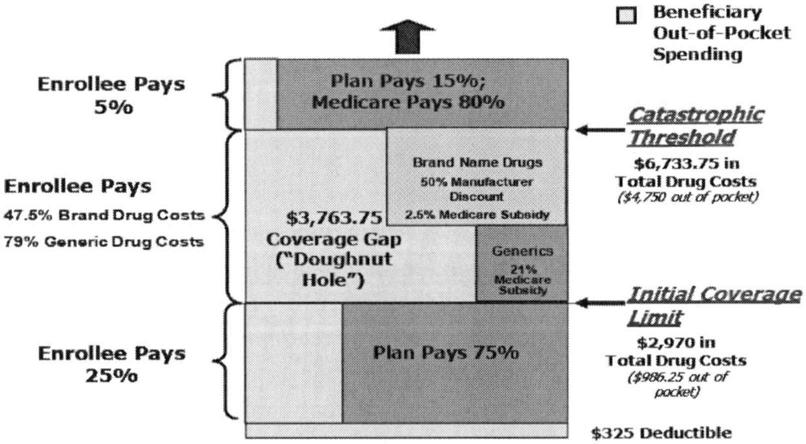

Source: Figure by CRS based on data from CMS, Announcement of CY 2013 Medicare Advantage Capitation Rates and Medicare Advantage and Part D Payment Policies and Final Call Letter, Attachments IV and V.

Figure 2. 2013 Standard Medicare Prescription Drug Benefit.

Medicare's payments to plans are determined through a competitive bidding process, and enrollee premiums are tied to plan bids. Plans are paid a risk-adjusted monthly per capita amount based on their bids during a given plan year. Part D plan sponsors determine payments for drugs and are expected to negotiate prices. The federal government is prohibited from interfering in the price negotiations between drug manufacturers, pharmacies, and plans (the so-called "non-interference clause").

Part D also provides enhanced coverage for low-income enrolled individuals, such as persons who previously received drug benefits under Medicaid (known as "dual eligibles"—enrollees in both Medicare and Medicaid). Additionally, certain persons who do not qualify for Medicaid, but whose incomes are below 150% of poverty, may also receive assistance for some portion of their premium and cost-sharing charges.

MMA included significant incentives for employers to continue to offer coverage to their retirees by providing a 28% federal subsidy. In 2013, the maximum potential subsidy per covered retiree is $1,757 for employers or unions offering drug coverage that is at least actuarially equivalent (called "creditable" coverage), to standard coverage.[50] Employers or unions may select an alternative option (instead of taking the subsidy) with respect to Part D, such as electing to pay a portion of the Part D premiums. They may also elect to provide enhanced coverage, though this has some financial consequences for the employer or union. Alternatively, employers or unions may contract with a PDP or MA-PD to offer the coverage or become a Part D plan sponsor themselves for their retirees.

ADMINISTRATION

CMS, a Department of Health and Human Services (HHS) operating division, administers the Medicare program.[51] CMS administers Medicare through contracts with private entities, such as Medicare Administrative Contractors (MACs). MACs help CMS run Medicare's day-to-day operations by paying reimbursement claims, processing provider and supplier enrollment applications, providing education and outreach, administering appeals, operating toll-free call centers, and other activities.

MMA required the Secretary to implement FFS contracting reform by 2011. CMS completed Round I of Parts A and B FFS contractor reform by awarding contracts to 15 A/B MACs to process Parts A and B claims and four DME MACs to process DME supplier claims. CMS plans to consolidate A/B MACs further to 10 contracts during a second round of contract awards, which began in July 2010 when CMS issued a request for information from interested bidders.[52] In 2012, CMS requested proposals from contractors for the second round of Medicare administrative contracts. CMS awarded new contracts in September 2012; however, unsuccessful bidders challenged CMS's contract award decisions.[53] GAO reviews contract challenges to determine if CMS followed appropriate contracting rules and procedures. Contract challenges can take a number of months to resolve; in the meantime, incumbent MACs continue to service the existing geographic areas.

In addition to MACs, CMS utilizes other private entities to assist with Medicare program operation activities.[54] CMS contracts with the following private organizations to protect the Medicare trust funds from making improper payments and to identify, recover, and where appropriate, prosecute, waste, fraud, and abuses: Recovery Audit Contractors (RACs), Zone Program Integrity Contractors (ZPICs), Medicare Drug Integrity Contractors (MEDICs), and Comprehensive Error Rate Testing (CERT) contractors.[55]

Under MMA Section 306, Congress authorized a three-year demonstration to test RACs in FFS Medicare Parts A and B, but based on early success, the demonstration was converted to a permanent program by the Section 302 of the Tax Relief and Healthcare Act of 2006 (TRHCA, P.L. 109-432). ACA further expanded RACs nationwide and applied them to all Medicare Parts (C and D, as well as A and B). Contracts were awarded to four private companies with territories that cover approximately one-quarter of the country.[56] RACs are responsible for reducing Medicare's improper payment rates by identifying underpayments and overpayments made to providers, recovering overpayments, and working with providers to prevent future improper payments. RACs are paid a contingency fee based on a percentage of the overpayments they recover from Medicare providers and suppliers. In FY2012, the Medicare RAC contractors identified approximately $2.4 billion in claims corrections, $2.3 billion of which were overpayments and $109 million were underpayments.[57]

In addition to Medicare program integrity enhancements in MMA and ACA, Section 4241 of the Small Business and Jobs Act of 2010 (SBJA, P.L. 111-240) appropriated $100 million for CMS to initiate predictive modeling and other analytics technologies ("predictive analytics technologies").[58] Predictive analytics technologies have been compared to technologies used in private sector financial services industries, such as banking, insurance, and credit cards, to reduce fraudulent billing. By combining data and information from multiple sources, including Medicare FFS claims history (aberrant billing patterns), enrollment information, background checks, other public and private information (links to questionable affiliations), and complaints, predictive analytics technologies could help to determine if claims were legitimate before they were paid. CMS awarded predictive modeling contracts in June 2011 to two private sector companies. In a report on the first year of the predictive modeling program, which CMS refers to as the Fraud Prevention System (FPS), CMS reported that approximately $115 million in potential FFS overpayments were prevented and there was a $3 to $1 return-on-investment over the first year.[59]

Medicare's quality assurance activities are handled by state Survey Agencies and Quality Improvement Organizations (QIOs), which operate in all states, the District of Columbia, Puerto Rico, and the U.S. Virgin Islands. State survey agencies are responsible for inspecting Medicare provider facilities (i.e., nursing homes, home health agencies, and hospitals) to ensure they are in compliance with federal safety and quality standards referred to as Conditions of Participation. QIOs monitor the quality of care delivered to Medicare beneficiaries and educate providers on the latest quality improvement techniques.

In January 2011, CMS established a Center for Medicare and Medicaid Innovation (CMI).[60] The purpose of CMMI is to test and evaluate innovative payment and service delivery models to reduce program expenditures under Medicare, Medicaid, and the State Children's Health Insurance Program (CHIP) while preserving or enhancing the quality of care furnished under these programs. In selecting the models, the Secretary is required to give preference to those that improve the coordination, quality, and efficiency of health care services.

FINANCING

Medicare's financial operations are accounted for through two trust funds maintained by the Department of the Treasury—the Hospital Insurance (HI) trust fund for Part A and the Supplementary Medical Insurance (SMI) trust fund for Parts B and D. For beneficiaries enrolled in Medicare Advantage (Part C), payments are made on their behalf in appropriate portions from the HI and SMI trust funds. HI is primarily funded by payroll taxes, while SMI is primarily funded through general revenue transfers and premiums. The HI and SMI trust funds are overseen by a Board of Trustees that provides annual reports to Congress.[61]

The trust funds are simply accounting mechanisms; there is no actual transfer of money into and out of a fund. Income to the trust funds is credited to the fund in the form of interest-bearing government securities. Expenditures for services and administrative costs are recorded against the fund. The securities represent obligations that the government has issued to itself. As long as a trust fund has a balance, the Treasury Department is authorized to make payments for it from the U.S. Treasury.

Medicare is primarily mandatory spending—generally Medicare pays for all covered health care services provided to beneficiaries. Aside from certain constraints in HI described below, the program is not subject to spending limits. Additionally, most Medicare expenditures (aside from premiums paid by beneficiaries) are paid for by current workers through ordinary income taxes and dedicated Medicare payroll taxes, that is, current income is used to pay current expenditures. Medicare taxes paid by current workers are not set aside to cover their future Medicare expenses.

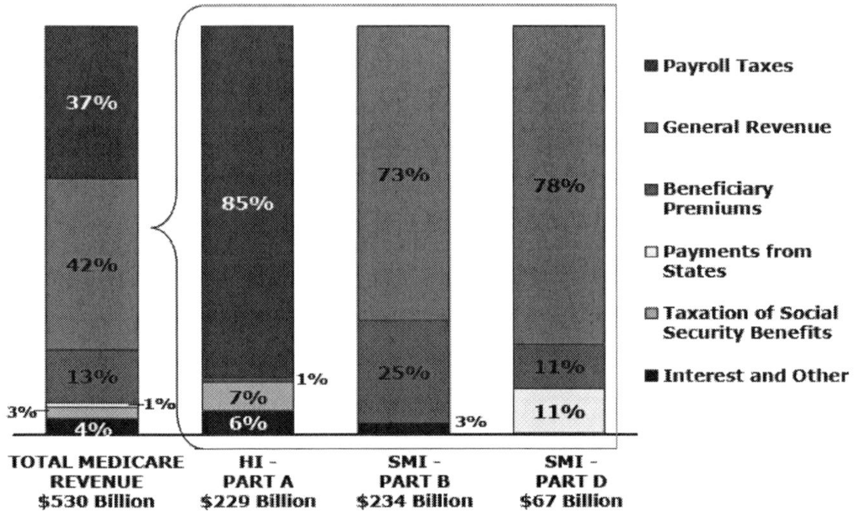

Source: 20 12 Report of the Medicare Trustees, Table II.B 1.
Notes: Totals may not add to 100% due to rounding.

Figure 3. Sources of Medicare Revenue: 2011.

Part A Financing

The primary source of funding for Part A is payroll taxes paid by employees and employers. Each pays a tax of 1.45% on the employee's earnings; the self-employed pay 2.9%. Beginning in 2013, some higher-income employees pay higher payroll taxes.[62] Unlike Social Security, there is no upper limit on earnings subject to the tax. Other sources of income include (1) interest on federal securities held by the trust fund, (2) a portion of federal income taxes that individuals pay on their social security benefits, (3) premiums paid by voluntary enrollees who are not automatically entitled to Medicare Part A, (4) transfers from states, and (5) other revenues. Income for Part A is credited to the HI trust fund. Part A expenditures for CY2013 are estimated to reach approximately $280 billion.[63] About $224 billion of this amount is expected to be funded by payroll taxes and $38 billion by interest income and other sources; approximately $18 billion will need to be drawn out of accumulated assets in the HI trust fund to make up the difference between expected income and expenditures.

As long as the HI trust fund has a balance, the Treasury Department is authorized to make payments for Medicare Part A services. To date, the HI trust fund has never run out of money (i.e., become insolvent), and there are no provisions in the Social Security Act that govern what would happen if that were to occur.

Since 2008, Part A expenditures have exceeded HI income each year, and the assets credited to the trust fund have been drawn down to make up the deficit. The 2012 report of the Medicare Board of Trustees estimates that under current law the HI trust fund will become insolvent in 2024 (i.e., the balance of the trust fund will reach $0), at which time there will no longer be sufficient funds to fully cover Part A expenditures.[64]

Part B Financing

Medicare Part B is financed mostly from federal general revenues, with beneficiary premiums set at 25% of estimated program costs for the aged. (The disabled pay the same premium as the aged.) Income for Part B is credited to the SMI trust fund.

Total spending for Part B is estimated to reach about $239 billion in CY2013, with general revenues financing approximately $194 billion of that amount.[65]

The 2013 monthly premium is $104.90 for most Medicare beneficiaries who voluntarily enroll in Part B. Individuals receiving Social Security benefits have their Part B premium payments automatically deducted from their Social Security benefit checks. An individual's Social Security check cannot go down from one year to the next as a result of the annual Part B premium increase (except in the case of higher-income individuals subject to income-related premiums).[66]

Since 2007, higher-income enrollees pay higher premiums.[67] In 2013, individuals whose modified adjusted gross income (AGI) exceeds $85,000 and each member of a couple filing jointly whose modified AGI exceeds $170,000 are subject to higher premium amounts. These higher-income premiums range from 35% to 80% of the value of Part B, affecting about 4% of Medicare Part B enrollees in 2012.[68]

As a result of ACA, the income thresholds have been frozen at the 2010 level through 2019, which means that more people may be subject to the high-income premium over time.

Part C Financing

Payments for spending under the Medicare Advantage program are made in appropriate portions from the HI and SMI trust funds. There is no separate trust fund for Part C.

Part D Financing

Medicare Part D is financed through a combination of beneficiary premiums and federal general revenues. In addition, certain transfers are made from the states. These transfers, referred to as "clawback payments," represent a portion of the amounts states could otherwise have been expected to pay for drugs under Medicaid if drug coverage for the dual eligible population had not been transferred to Part D. Part D revenues are credited to a separate Part D account within the SMI trust fund. In CY2013, total spending for Part D is estimated to reach approximately $79 billion, with about $60 billion of that amount paid for by general revenues.[69]

In 2013, the base beneficiary premium is $31.17;[70] however, beneficiaries pay different premiums depending on the plan they have selected and whether they are entitled to low-income premium subsidies. Additionally, beginning in 2011, higher income Part D enrollees pay higher premiums.[71] (The income thresholds are the same as for Part B, as described above.) On average, beneficiary premiums are set at 25.5% of expected total Part D costs for basic coverage.

Additional Insurance Coverage

While Medicare provides broad protection against the costs of many, primarily acute care, services, the program does not cover all services that may be used by its aged and disabled beneficiaries. For example, Medicare does not cover eyeglasses, hearing aids, dentures, or most long-term care services. Further, unlike most private insurance policies, it does not include an annual "catastrophic" cap on out-of-pocket spending on cost-sharing charges for services covered under Parts A and B (except for persons enrolled in Medicare Advantage plans).

Most Medicare beneficiaries have some coverage in addition to Medicare. The following are the main sources of additional coverage for Medicare enrollees.

- Medicare Advantage. Many MA plans offer services in addition to those covered under original Medicare, reduced cost sharing, or reduced Part B or D premiums. All MA plans have a catastrophic cap.[72]
- Employer Coverage. Coverage may be provided through a current or former employer. In recent years, a number of employers have cut back on the scope of retiree coverage. Some have dropped such coverage entirely, particularly for future retirees. As noted earlier, the MMA attempted to stem this trend, at least for prescription drug coverage, by offering subsidies to employers who offer drug coverage, at least as good as that available under Part D.
- Medigap.[73] Individual insurance policies that supplement fee-for-service Medicare are referred to as Medigap policies. Beneficiaries with Medigap insurance typically have coverage for a portion of Medicare's deductibles and coinsurance; they may also have coverage for some items and services not covered by Medicare. Individuals select from a set of standardized plans, though not all plans are offered in all states.
- Medicaid. Certain low-income Medicare beneficiaries also may be eligible for full or partial benefits under their state's Medicaid program.[74] Individuals eligible for both Medicare and Medicaid are referred to as dual eligibles. The lowest-income dual eligibles qualify for full Medicaid benefits, so that the majority of their health care expenses are paid by either Medicare or Medicaid; Medicare pays first, with Medicaid picking up most of the remaining costs. In addition to full-benefit dual eligibles, state Medicaid programs pay Medicare premiums and some cost-sharing for other partial dual eligibles, who have higher income than full-benefit dual eligibles but are still considered to have low income.[75]
- Other Public Sources. Individuals may have additional coverage through the Department of Veterans Affairs, or TRICARE for military retirees eligible for Medicare (and enrolled in Part B).

In 2009, about 93% of Medicare beneficiaries had some form of additional coverage. (Some persons may have had more than one type of additional coverage.)

APPENDIX A. ACRONYMS

ACA	Patient Protection and Affordable Care Act, as modified by the Health Care and Education Reconciliation Act of 2010 (P.L. 111-148 and P.L. 111-152)
ACO	Accountable Care Organization
AGI	Adjusted Gross Income
APC	Ambulatory Payment Classification
ASC	Ambulatory Surgical Center
ASP	Average Sales Price
ATRA	American Taxpayer Relief Act of 2012 (P.L. 112-240)
BBA 97	Balanced Budget Act of 1997 (P.L. 105-33)
BBRA	Medicare, Medicaid, and SCHIP Balanced Budget Refinement Act of 1999 (P.L. 113)
BCA	Budget Control Act of 2011 (P.L. 112-25)
BIPA	Medicare, Medicaid and SCHIP Benefits Improvement and Protection Act of 2000 (P.L. 106-554)
CAH	Critical Access Hospital
CBO	Congressional Budget Office
CMI	Center for Medicare and Medicaid Innovation
CMS	Centers for Medicare & Medicaid Services
CORF	Comprehensive Outpatient Rehabilitation Facility
CPI	Consumer Price Index
CPI-U	Consumer Price Index for Urban Consumers
DGME	Direct Graduate Medical Education
DME	Durable Medical Equipment
DMEPOS	Durable Medical Equipment, Prosthetics, Orthotics, and Other Medical Supplies
DRA	Deficit Reduction Act of 2005 (P.L. 109-171)
DRG	Diagnosis Related Group
DSH	Disproportionate Share Hospital
ESRD	End-Stage Renal Disease
FFS	Fee-for-Service
FPL	Federal Poverty Level
FQHC	Federally Qualified Health Center
GAO	Government Accountability Office
GDP	Gross Domestic Product

GME	Graduate Medical Education
HCERA	Health Care and Education Reconciliation Act of 2010 (P.L. 111-152)
HHA	Home Health Agency
HHRG	Home Health Resource Group
HHS	Department of Health and Human Services
HI	Hospital Insurance (Medicare Part A)
HMO	Health Maintenance Organization
HOPD	Hospital Outpatient Department
IME	Indirect Medical Education
IPAB	Independent Payment Advisory Board
IPF	Inpatient Psychiatric Facility
IPPS	Inpatient Prospective Payment System
IRF	Inpatient Rehabilitation Facility
LIS	Low-Income Subsidy
LTC	Long-Term Care
LTCH	Long-Term Care Hospital
MA	Medicare Advantage
MA-PD	Medicare Advantage – Prescription Drug (Plan)
MAC	Medicare Administrative Contractor
MCTRJCA	Middle Class Tax Relief and Job Creation Act of 2012
MedPAC	Medicare Payment Advisory Commission
MEI	Medical Economic Index
MIPPA	Medicare Improvements for Patients and Providers Act of 2008 (P.L. 110-275)
MMA	Medicare Prescription Drug Improvement and Modernization Act of 2003 (P.L 108-173)
MMSEA	Medicare, Medicaid and SCHIP Extension Act of 2007 (P.L. 110-173)
MS-DRG	Medicare Severity Diagnosis Related Groups
MSP	Medicare Savings Program
OIG	Office of Inspector General
OMB	Office of Management and Budget
OPPS	Outpatient Prospective Payment System
PDP	Prescription Drug Plan
PFFS	Private Fee-for-Service
PO	Prosthetics and Orthotics
PPS	Prospective Payment System
QI	Qualified Individual
QIO	Quality Improvement Organization
QMB	Qualified Medicare Beneficiary
RAC	Recovery Audit Contractor
RBRVS	Resource-Based Relative Value Scale
RHC	Rural Health Clinic
RUG	Resource Utilization Group

Appendix A. (Continued)

SCH	Sole Community Hospital
SGR	Sustainable Growth Rate
SLMB	Specified Low-Income Beneficiaries
SMI	Supplementary Medical Insurance (Medicare Parts B and D)
SNF	Skilled Nursing Facility
SNP	Special Needs Plan
SSA	Social Security Act
SSI	Supplemental Security Income
TRHCA	Tax Relief and Health Care Act of 2006 (P.L. 109-432)
USPSTF	United States Preventative Services Task Force

APPENDIX B. 2013 MEDICARE BENEFICIARY COSTS

Table B-1. Part A (Hospitalization Insurance) 2013 Premiums, Deductible and Additional Cost-Sharing

Premiums	
Individuals with:	2013 Monthly Premium
40 or more quarters of Social Security credits	$0
30 -39 quarters of Social Security credits	$243
0 - 29 quarters of Social Security credits	$441
Deductible and Additional Cost-Sharing	
Inpatient Hospital	
Deductible	$1,184 per benefit period
Days 1-60	No coinsurance
Days 61-90	$296 per day
Days 91-150	$592 per day (for up to 60 lifetime reserve days)
After 150 Days	Beneficiary pays 100%
Skilled Nursing Facility (SNF)	
Days 1-20	No coinsurance
Days 21-100	$148 per day
After 100 Days	Beneficiary pays 100%
Home Health	No coinsurance
Hospice	No coinsurance for hospice care; copayment of up to $5 per outpatient drug prescription

Table B-2. Part B (Supplementary Medical Insurance) 2013 Premiums, Deductible and Additional Cost-Sharing

Premiums		
Yearly income in 2011 (2012 Tax Return)		
File Individual Tax Return	File *Joint Tax Return*	2013 Monthly Premium[a]
$85,000 or less	$170,000 or less	$104.90
above $85,000 up to $107,000	above $170,000 up to $214,000	$146.90
above $107,000 up to $160,000	above $214,000 up to $320,000	$209.80
above $160,000 up to $214,000	above $320,000 up to $428,000	$272.70
above $214,000	above $428,000	$335.70
Deductible		
Deductible		$147 per year
Additional Cost-Sharing		
Physician and Non-Physician Practitioner Services	20% co-insurance, plus up to an additional 15% of the amount if the medical provider does not accept assignment	
Outpatient Hospital Care	20% coinsurance	
Ambulatory Surgical Services	20% coinsurance	
Durable Medical Equipment	20% coinsurance	
Physical, Occupational, and Speech Therapy	20% coinsurance, certain limits may apply	
Clinical Laboratory Services	No coinsurance, deductible does not apply	
Home Health	No coinsurance, deductible does not apply	
Outpatient Mental Health Services	35% coinsurance (phasing down to 20% in 2014)	
Certain Preventive Services	No coinsurance	

[a] May be higher if enrolled late in Part B.

Table B-3. Part C (Medicare Advantage)

Premiums, deductibles and additional cost-sharing vary by plan. (See http://www.medicare.gov/find-a-plan for plan premiums.)

Table B-4. Part D (Outpatient Prescription Drug Benefit) 2013 Premiums, Deductible and Additional Cost-Sharing

Premiums		
Premiums vary by plan. (See http://www.medicare.gov/find-a-plan for plan premiums.) Higher income beneficiaries pay an income-related monthly adjustment amount in addition to their plan premiums. Beneficiaries who receive the lowincome subsidy generally pay no premium.		
Yearly income in 2011 (2012 Tax Return)		
File *Individual Tax Return*	File *Joint Tax Return*	2013 Monthly Premiuma
$85,000 or less	$170,000 or less	Plan Premium
above $85,000 up to $107,000	above $170,000 up to $214,000	Plan Premium + $11.60
above $107,000 up to $160,000	above $214,000 up to $320,000	Plan Premium + $29.90
above $160,000 up to $214,000	above $320,000 up to $428,000	Plan Premium + $48.30
above $214,000	above $428,000	Plan Premium + $66.60
Deductible and Additional Cost-Sharing		
The amounts below apply to the standard Part D benefit; actual benefits and cost-sharing requirements may vary by plan. Beneficiaries receiving low-income subsidies pay reduced cost-sharing amounts.		
Deductible	$325	
Initial Coverage (up to $2,970 in total drug costs)	25% coinsurance	
Coverage Gap (between $2,970 and approximately $6,733.75 in total drug costs)	Beneficiary pays 79% of the cost of generic drugs; and 47.5% of brand name drugs.	
Catastrophic Coverage (above $4,750 in beneficiary out-of-pocket spending)	Minimum of $2.65 for generic drugs, $6.60 for brand drugs; or 5% coinsurance.	

[a] May be higher if enrolled late in Part D.

End Notes

[1] Appendix A provides a list of commonly used acronyms in this report, including acronyms for Public Laws.

[2] CBO February 2013 Medicare Baseline, http://www.cbo.gov/sites/default/files/cbofiles /attachments/ 43894_Medicare2.pdf.

[3] Also known as "customary, prevailing and reasonable charges," this method based physician payments on charges commonly used by physicians in a local community. The payment for

a service was the lowest of (1) the physician's billed charge for the service, (2) the physician's customary charge for the service, or (3) the prevailing charge for that service in the community.

[4] ESRD is a stage of kidney impairment that appears to be irreversible and permanent, requiring a regular course of dialysis treatments or a kidney transplantation to maintain life.

[5] For additional information on major legislative changes to Medicare from 1997 through 2012, see Chapter 2 of the House Committee on Ways and Means *2012 Greenbook* at http://greenbook.waysandmeans.house.gov/2012-greenbook/chapter-2-medicare.

[6] For more information, see CRS Report RL31966, *Overview of the Medicare Prescription Drug, Improvement, and Modernization Act of 2003*.

[7] See CRS Report R40082, *Medicare: Part B Premiums*, by Patricia A. Davis.

[8] See CRS Report RS22796, *Medicare Trigger*, by Patricia A. Davis, Christopher M. Davis, and Todd Garvey.

[9] For more information, see CRS Report RL34360, *P.L. 110-173: Provisions in the Medicare, Medicaid, and SCHIP Extension Act of 2007*.

[10] For more information, see CRS Report RL34592, *P.L. 110-275: The Medicare Improvements for Patients and Providers Act of 2008*.

[11] For more information, see CRS Report R41196, *Medicare Provisions in the Patient Protection and Affordable Care Act (PPACA): Summary and Timeline*, and CRS General Distribution Memorandum, *Estimates of Medicare Savings in the Patient Protection and Affordable Care Act*, by Patricia A Davis, August 31, 2012, available upon request.

[12] See CRS Report R41511, *The Independent Payment Advisory Board*, by Jim Hahn and Christopher M. Davis.

[13] Groups of providers and suppliers who work together to manage and coordinate care for Medicare fee-for-service beneficiaries. See CRS Report R41474, *Accountable Care Organizations and the Medicare Shared Savings Program*, by Amanda K. Sarata.

[14] For a comprehensive discussion of the BCA, see CRS Report R41965, *The Budget Control Act of 2011*, by Bill Heniff Jr., Elizabeth Rybicki, and Shannon M. Mahan.

[15] For additional information, see CRS Report R42884, *The "Fiscal Cliff" and the American Taxpayer Relief Act of 2012*, coordinated by Mindy R. Levit.

[16] Section 256(d) of the Balanced Budget and Emergency Deficit Control Act of 1985 (BBEDCA, P.L. 99-177) contains special rules for the Medicare program in case of a sequestration. While BBEDCA ordinarily limits reduction of certain Medicare spending to 4% under a sequestration order, the BCA limits the size of this reduction to 2%. See CRS Report R42050, *Budget "Sequestration" and Selected Program Exemptions and Special Rules*, coordinated by Karen Spar for additional detail.

[17] OMB will determine which parts of the Medicare program fall under the 2% cap and which could be subject to higher caps.

[18] Congressional Budget Office, *Estimated Impact of Automatic Budget Enforcement Procedures Specified in the Budget Control Act*, September 12, 2011, http://www.cbo.gov/ftpdocs /124xx/doc12414/09-12-BudgetControlAct.pdf.

[19] For more information, see CRS Report RS22195, *Social Security Disability Insurance (SSDI) and Medicare: The 24- Month Waiting Period for SSDI Beneficiaries Under Age 65*, by Scott Szymendera.

[20] See CRS Report R40082, *Medicare: Part B Premiums*, by Patricia A. Davis.

[21] Starting in 2011, MA enrollees are only permitted to drop out of their MA plans and return to original Medicare during the first 45-day period of each calendar year. Though they are no longer allowed to switch to another MA plan as they were able to do previously, MA

enrollees who use the 45-day period to disenroll from their MA plan may enroll in a stand-alone Part D prescription drug plan (PDP), or may elect to enroll in other non-Medicare Advantage private plan options, such as a Medicare Cost plan or a demonstration plan. MA enrollees will still be able to switch plans during special enrollment periods, such as when an MA enrollee moves outside his or her plan's service area or if an enrollee's MA plan is terminated.

[22] In addition to the yearly Medicare & You Handbook, http://www.medicare.gov/publications /pubs/pdf/10050.pdf, which is mailed to beneficiaries' homes, beneficiaries can consult http://www.Medicare.gov to find information such as the items and services covered under Medicare, cost sharing requirements, participating medical providers and private health plan, and nursing home quality scores.

[23] If a Medicare beneficiary enrolls in a Private Fee-for-Service (PFFS) plan that does not provide drug coverage, he or she may enroll in a stand-alone Prescription Drug Plan (PDP). However, enrollees in other types of MA plans who want Part D prescription drug coverage must choose a Medicare Advantage Prescription Drug (MA-PD) plan, which is an MA plan that provides all Medicare required parts A, B, and D benefits. If a Medicare beneficiary enrolls in a local HMO or regional PPO that does not offer drug coverage, he or she does not have the option to enroll in a stand-alone PDP plan.

[24] For additional information on enrollment periods see Medicare Publication "Understanding Medicare Enrollment Periods," at http://www.medicare.gov/Publications /Pubs/pdf /11219.pdf.

[25] Hospitals in the state of Maryland are exempt from the IPPS and are paid under a state-specific payment system.

[26] For additional information on skilled nursing facility benefits, see CRS Report R42401, *Medicare's Skilled Nursing Facility Primer: Benefit Basics and Issues*, by Scott R. Talaga.

[27] By October 1, 2013, the Secretary will be required to implement budget neutral revisions to the methodology for determining hospice payments for routine home care and other services. These revisions could include adjustments to the per diem payments reflecting differences in resources used during the course of an entire episode of hospice care.

[28] For details, see the Annual Reports of the Board of Trustees of the Federal Hospital Insurance and Federal Supplementary Medical Insurance Trust Funds, http://www.cms.hhs.gov /reportstrustfunds/.

[29] Certain durable medical equipment suppliers in competitive bidding areas are required to accept assignment.

[30] This "mental health parity" was introduced in MIPPA (P.L. 110-275). Beneficiaries are responsible for a 35% copayment for outpatient mental health services in 2013.

[31] For details, see CRS Report R40907, *Medicare Physician Payment Updates and the Sustainable Growth Rate (SGR) System*, by Jim Hahn and Janemarie Mulvey.

[32] The Temporary Payroll Tax Cut Continuation Act of 2011 (P.L. 112-78) included an override of the statutory SGR update for January and February 2012, and the Middle Class Tax Relief and Job Creation Act of 2012 (MCTRJCA, P.L. 112-96) maintained the payment freeze through the end of 2012.

[33] See CRS Report R42944, *Medicare, Medicaid, and Other Health Provisions in the American Taxpayer Relief Act of 2012*, coordinated by Jim Hahn.

[34] For details, see CRS Report R41196, *Medicare Provisions in the Patient Protection and Affordable Care Act (PPACA): Summary and Timeline*, coordinated by Patricia A. Davis.

[35] The MCTRJCA and ATRA applied the cap and threshold to therapy services furnished in hospital outpatient departments and critical access hospitals in 2012 and 2013.

[36] Social Security Act §1862(a)(1)(A); 42 U.S.C. 1395y(a)(1)(A).

[37] U.S. Preventive Services Task Force, http://www.uspreventiveservicestaskforce.org/.

[38] A complete list of covered services, intervals, and limitations is available at CMS, overview of Medicare prevention, http://www.cms.gov/Medicare/Prevention/Prevntion GenInfo/index.html.

[39] See CMS Medicare Learning Network Matters Number MM8132, "Calendar Year (CY) 2013 Annual Update for Clinical Laboratory Fee Schedule and Laboratory Services Subject to Reasonable Charge Payment," at http://www.cms.gov/Outreach-and-Education/Medicare-Learning-Network-MLN/MLNMattersArticles/Downloads/ MM8132.pdf.

[40] See General Accounting Office (GAO) report, "Medicare Payments for Oxygen," May 15, 1997, GAO-97-120R; HHS Office of the Inspector General report, "Medicare Home Oxygen Equipment: Cost and Servicing," September 2006, OEI-09-04-00420.

[41] For more information, see CRS Report R41211, *Medicare Durable Medical Equipment: The Competitive Bidding Program*, by Paulette C. Morgan.

[42] Biologics are generally derived from living organisms rather than inorganic chemical compounds.

[43] Additionally, starting in 2006, rural sole community hospitals (SCHs) receive an additional 7.1% in Medicare payments. Special payment protections apply to cancer hospitals, children's hospitals, small rural hospitals (that are not SCHs) with 100 or fewer beds, and SCHs.

[44] New, office-based procedures are services that are performed in physician offices at least 50% of the time. Payment is set at the lower of the ASC rate or the practice expense portion of the physician fee schedule payment rate.

[45] Under certain circumstances, Part B will cover an non-emergency ambulance service during a Part A covered stay, including transport of a skilled nursing facility (SNF) resident with end-stage renal disease to and from a dialysis facility for dialysis services.

[46] For additional information, see CRS Report RL30526, *Medicare Payment Updates and Payment Rates*, coordinated by Paulette C. Morgan.

[47] The Part D program was created by the Medicare Prescription Drug, Improvement, and Modernization Act of 2003 (P.L. 108-173), and began in 2006.

[48] The actual level of total covered Part D spending before reaching the catastrophic threshold will depend on whether the individual qualifies for the low-income subsidy and the portion of brand name and generic drugs purchased during the coverage gap.

[49] For additional information, see CRS Report R41196, *Medicare Provisions in the Patient Protection and Affordable Care Act (PPACA): Summary and Timeline*, coordinated by Patricia A. Davis.

[50] The ACA changed how these subsidies are treated for tax purposes. Originally, MMA allowed employers to exclude the retiree drug subsidies from their gross income, as well as claim a business deduction for retiree prescription drug expenses. Beginning in 2013, the allowed deduction for retiree prescription drug coverage is reduced by the amount of the federal drug subsidy received. For additional information, see CRS Report R41128, *Health-Related Revenue Provisions in the Patient Protection and Affordable Care Act (ACA)*, by Janemarie Mulvey.

[51] The Department of Health and Human Services organization chart is available at http://www.hhs.gov/about/orgchart/. CMS's organization chart is at http://www.cms.gov /About-CMS/Agency-Information/CMSLeadership/downloads/ CMS_Organizational_Chart.pdf.

[52] For more information, see http://www.cms.gov/MedicareContractingReform/02_Spotlight.asp#TopOfPage.

[53] For more information on the current status of CMS's round 2 MAC rebids, see http://www.cms.gov/MedicareMedicare-Contracting/MedicareContractingReform/Spotlight.html.

[54] Most program integrity authority was originally provided in the Health Insurance Portability and Accountability Act of 1996 (HIPAA, P.L. 104-191), although a number of other laws have added fraud and abuse authority and sustained HIPAA's funding.

[55] For more information on Medicare contractors and Medicare fraud and abuse, see CRS Report RL34217, *Medicare Program Integrity: Activities to Protect Medicare from Payment Errors, Fraud, and Abuse*, by Cliff Binder.

[56] The four FFS RACs are Region A: Diversified Collections Services, Region B: CGI, Inc., Region C: Connolly, Inc., and Region D: HealthDataInsights.

[57] The Centers for Medicare & Medicaid Services, FY2011 Fee-for-Service Recovery Audit Program, November 2012, https://www.cms.gov/Research-Statistics-Data-and-Systems/Monitoring-Programs/Recovery-Audit-Program/ Downloads/National-Program-Corrections-FY-2012-4th-Qtr-2012.pdf.

[58] Section 4241, "Use of Predictive Modeling and other Analytic Technologies to Identify and Prevent Waste, Fraud, and Abuse in the Medicare Fee-for-Service Program," of the Small Business and Jobs Act of 2010 (P.L. 111-240) authorized a one-time $100 million appropriation from the Medicare Trust Funds. The predictive modeling funding is available until expended. If certain interim objectives are not met by the predictive modeling program, the Secretary may impose moratoriums on further expansion, until refinements or improvements are made.

[59] Ibid.

[60] For more information, see http://innovations.cms.gov/.

[61] For more information on Medicare financing, see CRS Report R41436, *Medicare Financing*, by Patricia A. Davis.

[62] For additional information, see Internal Revenue Service, *Questions and Answers for the Additional Medicare Tax*, at http://www.irs.gov/Businesses/Small-Businesses-&-Self-Employed/Questions-and-Answers-for-the-AdditionalMedicare-Tax.

[63] 2012 Annual Report of the Boards of Trustees of the Federal Hospital Insurance and Federal Supplementary Medical Insurance Trust Funds, Table III.B4, p. 60, http://www.cms.hhs.gov/reportstrustfunds/. Note, the Medicare trustees generally report expenditures on a calendar year basis, while CBO reports on a fiscal year basis.

[64] For additional information on HI solvency estimates, see CRS Report RS20946, *Medicare: History of Insolvency Projections*, by Patricia A. Davis.

[65] 2012 Annual Report of the Boards of Trustees of the Federal Hospital Insurance and Federal Supplementary Medical Insurance Trust Funds, Table III.C4, p. 98, http://www.cms.hhs.gov/reportstrustfunds/.

[66] See CRS Report R40082, *Medicare: Part B Premiums*, by Patricia A. Davis, and CRS Report R40561, *Interactions Between the Social Security COLA and Medicare Part B Premiums*, by Jim Hahn.

[67] For additional information, see Social Security publication, *Medicare Premiums: Rules for Higher-Income Beneficiaries*, http://www.ssa.gov/pubs/10536.pdf.

[68] The higher monthly premium amounts for 2013 are based on 2011 income levels and are (1) $146.90—for single beneficiaries with income $85,001-$107,000 or for each member of a couple filing jointly with income $170,001- $214,000; (2) $209.80—for single beneficiaries

with income $107,001-$160,000 or for each member of a couple filing jointly with income $214,001-$320,000; (3) $272.70—for single beneficiaries with incomes $160,001-$214,000 and each member of a couple filing jointly with income $320,001-$428,000; and (4) $335.70—for single beneficiaries with incomes greater than $214,000 and each member of a couple filing jointly income above $428,000.

[69] 2012 Annual Report of the Boards of Trustees of the Federal Hospital Insurance and Federal Supplementary Medical Insurance Trust Funds, Table III.D3, p. 122, http://www.cms.hhs.gov/reportstrustfunds/.

[70] There is no "hold harmless" provision under Part D similar to that under Part B. Part D premium increases are not affected by Social Security cost-of-living adjustments.

[71] For additional information, see Social Security publication, *Medicare Premiums: Rules for Higher-Income Beneficiaries*, http://www.ssa.gov/pubs/10536.pdf.

[72] Starting in 2011, all MA plans are required to include a maximum out-of-pocket (OOP) limit determined by CMS. Prior to 2011, only MA regional plans were required to include a catastrophic cap on OOP spending.

[73] See CRS Report R42745, *Medigap: A Primer*, by Carol Rapaport.

[74] See CRS Report RL33202, *Medicaid: A Primer*, by Elicia J. Herz for additional information.

[75] In addition to individuals eligible for full Medicaid benefits, other low-income Medicare beneficiaries are entitled to limited benefits under the Medicare Savings Program (MSP). MSP includes three benefit categories each with different benefit levels: (1) Qualified Medicare Beneficiaries (QMBs), (2) Specified Low-Income Beneficiaries (SLMB), and (3) Qualified Individuals (QIs). For QMBs, state Medicaid programs pay Medicare Part B premiums and Medicare cost-sharing (deductibles and co-payments) when beneficiaries' incomes are under 100% of the federal poverty level (FPL). For SLMBs, state Medicaid programs pay Part B premiums when beneficiaries' incomes are between 100% and 120% of the FPL. For QIs, Medicaid pays premiums when beneficiaries' incomes are between 120% and 135% of poverty. To be eligible for MSP, Medicare beneficiaries must also meet Medicaid's other eligibility requirements (e.g., meet citizenship or legal residency requirements).

INDEX

A

abuse, 89, 124
access, 91, 94, 99, 104, 105, 122
accounting, viii, 2, 85, 111
acid, 61, 63
adenocarcinoma, 68
adjustment, 8, 13, 14, 15, 16, 17, 20, 34, 37, 40, 73, 93, 94, 98, 100, 120
administrative costs, ix, 84, 85, 111
age, viii, 2, 4, 7, 9, 10, 11, 12, 13, 36, 37, 47, 50, 51, 52, 53, 58, 59, 67, 75, 90, 97
agencies, 95, 99, 110
Alaska, 19, 41
ALS, ix, 37, 83, 90, 104
amyotrophic lateral sclerosis, ix, 83, 90
anemia, 50, 52, 62, 68, 69, 75, 81, 96, 102
antibody, 62, 78
anti-cancer, 102
APC, 102, 103, 116
APCs, 102, 103
appropriations, ix, 84, 85
arterial hypertension, 54, 58, 61, 62, 69, 75, 76
arthritis, 61, 77
assessment, 96
assets, 13, 18, 27, 42, 112, 113
asthma, 57, 61, 74
audit, ix, 84
authority, 10, 124

B

banking, 110
base, 80, 94, 96, 114
base rate, 96
benchmarks, 106
benefits, viii, ix, 2, 3, 4, 6, 9, 11, 12, 15, 18, 20, 21, 22, 24, 28, 36, 37, 39, 41, 42, 43, 49, 81, 84, 85, 86, 87, 88, 89, 90, 91, 105, 106, 107, 108, 112, 113, 115, 120, 122, 125
bleeding, 80, 81
blood, 49, 51, 58, 60, 61, 75, 76, 80, 81, 100, 101
blood clot, 49, 80, 81
body mass index, 97
bonds, 19
bone, 53, 61, 63, 76, 80
bone marrow, 61, 76, 80
bone marrow transplant, 61, 76
bonuses, 14
brachytherapy, 103
breathing, 57, 61, 74
browser, 38
Budget Committee, 43
budget deficit, 89

C

calcium, 63, 76
call centers, 109
cancer, 48, 49, 50, 51, 56, 59, 61, 63, 75, 76, 81, 90, 94, 123
candidates, 67
carcinoid tumor, 62, 77
cash, 4, 11, 13, 90
category a, 94
Census, 47
CFR, 38, 39
challenges, 109
chemical, 52, 123
chemotherapy, 51, 53, 58, 59, 60, 61, 75, 76, 77, 102
children, 94, 123
chronic kidney XE "kidney" disease, 51, 52, 53, 56, 58, 60, 62, 63, 66, 73, 75, 79, 81
chronic lymphocytic leukemia, 62, 67, 68, 78
chronic obstructive pulmonary disease, 57, 59, 74
citizenship, 125
civil service, 11
classification, 94, 102, 103
coding, 63
color, iv
colorectal cancer, 100
colostomy, 101
commercial, 46
Committees on Appropriations, 86
community, 93, 121, 123
complexity, 53
compliance, 110
compounds, 123
Congress, iv, viii, ix, 2, 4, 14, 25, 28, 37, 84, 85, 88, 89, 98, 100, 110, 111
congressional action, ix, 84
Congressional Budget Office, 40, 85, 86, 106, 116, 121
Consolidated Appropriations Act, 43
consumer price index, 18, 28
Consumer Price Index, 20, 28, 95, 116
consumers, 18, 95
contingency, 12, 13, 14, 35, 42, 110
coordination, 105, 111
counseling, 37
covered services, ix, 84, 85, 87, 92, 97, 99, 105, 123
covering, 28
CPI, 18, 20, 22, 24, 41, 95, 100, 116
cyclophosphamide, 67

D

damages, iv
database, 46, 47
deduction, 11, 39, 85, 123
deficiency, 62, 75
deficit, 113
deflation, 21
DEFRA, 30
dentures, 114
Department of Defense, 80
Department of Health and Human Services, 46, 84, 109, 117, 123
Department of the Treasury, 111
depression, 100
diabetes, 104
dialysis, ix, 37, 81, 83, 90, 96, 121, 123
diarrhea, 54, 62, 77
direct cost, 93
direct costs, 93
disability, ix, 3, 4, 6, 9, 10, 11, 37, 43, 69, 83, 90
disabled persons, vii, 1, 2, 7, 8, 19, 39, 90
discharges, 93
disease progression, 68
diseases, 49, 62, 78, 80, 81
disorder, 80, 81
District of Columbia, 110
DME, 46, 48, 49, 80, 101, 102, 109, 116
doctors, 87, 98
documentary evidence, 10

dosage, 73, 74
double counting, 47
dressings, 101
drugs, vii, viii, 14, 45, 46, 47, 48, 49, 50, 51, 52, 53, 54, 55, 56, 69, 73, 74, 80, 81, 92, 94, 96, 101, 102, 103, 104, 107, 108, 114, 120

E

earnings, 3, 24, 85, 90, 112
education, 93, 109
eligibility criteria, 18
emergency, 90, 104, 123
employees, 8, 9, 10, 38, 39, 91, 112
employers, 3, 38, 85, 87, 108, 112, 115, 123
employment, vii, ix, 1, 4, 8, 9, 12, 19, 36, 39, 83, 90, 91
end-stage renal disease, 10, 37, 50, 51, 53, 57, 59, 74, 87, 95, 123
enrollees, viii, ix, 2, 3, 4, 6, 12, 13, 14, 16, 18, 21, 22, 25, 30, 31, 33, 37, 42, 43, 84, 90, 91, 92, 97, 105, 106, 107, 108, 112, 113, 114, 115, 121, 122
enrollment, vii, 1, 2, 4, 5, 6, 7, 8, 9, 10, 12, 25, 36, 37, 38, 39, 43, 44, 90, 91, 100, 106, 109, 110, 122
enrollment penalty, vii, 1, 2, 6, 7, 8, 9, 10, 25, 43, 91, 92
Environmental Protection Agency, 90
EPA, 90
equipment, vii, 1, 3, 24, 46, 55, 73, 80, 92, 95, 96, 97, 101, 104, 122
erythropoietin, 102
ESRD, 10, 37, 50, 51, 52, 53, 57, 58, 59, 60, 63, 64, 65, 66, 72, 73, 74, 75, 79, 81, 87, 90, 96, 102, 105, 116, 121
ethnicity, 97
evidence, 47, 100

F

families, 80
FDA, 46, 49, 50, 51, 53, 54, 55, 58, 63, 66, 69, 70, 73, 79, 80, 81
federal general revenues, viii, ix, 2, 16, 84, 113, 114
federal government, 10, 20, 39, 41, 43, 105, 108
Federal Register, 17, 23, 31, 33, 34, 37, 39, 40, 43
financial, 86, 109, 110, 111
Food and Drug Administration, 46
formula, 14, 28, 42, 98
fraud, 89, 109, 124
freezing, 100
funding, 13, 26, 86, 112, 124
funds, 14, 19, 111, 113

G

GAO, 45, 47, 51, 52, 53, 54, 55, 58, 63, 66, 69, 70, 73, 79, 109, 116, 123
GDP, 2, 27, 85, 116
General Accounting Office, 123
generic drugs, 107, 120, 123
geography, 105
glaucoma, 100
glioblastoma, 67
glucocorticoids, 67
glucose, 101
goods and services, 41
government securities, 111
grants, 81
Gross Domestic Product, 116
growth, ix, 22, 24, 27, 28, 42, 68, 84, 88
growth factor, 68

H

Hawaii, 19, 41
Health and Human Services, 97

health care, vii, ix, 1, 2, 9, 18, 24, 26, 38, 46, 63, 80, 83, 84, 85, 87, 107, 111, 115
health care system, 80
health information, 14
health insurance, ix, 8, 9, 10, 37, 38, 47, 49, 63, 80, 83, 84, 87
health services, 43, 85, 92, 95, 96, 122
health status, viii, 2, 12, 38
heart disease, 100
heart failure, 54, 57, 61, 69, 75
hemophilia, 48, 49, 52
hepatitis, 48, 80, 100
HHS, 41, 84, 100, 109, 117, 123
high blood pressure, 54
high-priority issue, ix, 84, 85
history, 13, 19, 21, 49, 105, 110
HIV, 51, 52, 58, 60, 61, 75, 76
homes, 122
hospice, ix, 3, 83, 85, 92, 94, 95, 105, 118, 122
hospital insurance, vii, 43
House, 27, 43, 86, 121
human, 81
hypercalcemia, 68

I

idiopathic, 60, 62, 78
idiopathic thrombocytopenic purpura, 60, 62, 78
immune system, 52
immunodeficiency, 56, 60, 61, 62, 77, 78, 79
immunosuppressive drugs, 49, 102
improvements, 124
income, viii, 2, 3, 4, 8, 11, 12, 14, 15, 16, 17, 18, 19, 20, 21, 22, 24, 26, 27, 28, 30, 31, 37, 39, 40, 41, 42, 43, 87, 88, 89, 90, 91, 92, 93, 108, 111, 112, 113, 114, 115, 119, 120, 123, 124, 125
income levels, viii, 2, 16, 19, 124
income tax, 111, 112
individuals, vii, ix, 1, 2, 4, 7, 8, 9, 10, 11, 15, 16, 18, 19, 20, 21, 25, 36, 37, 38, 39, 42, 43, 80, 83, 84, 87, 90, 91, 95, 96, 106, 108, 112, 113, 125
industries, 110
infection, 51, 61, 76, 77
inflation, 18, 20, 22, 24, 28, 101, 104
influenza, 48, 52, 53, 62, 74, 78
influenza a, 52
influenza vaccine, 48, 52, 53, 74
ingredients, 102
injuries, 95
injury, iv, 100, 101
insurance policy, 19
integrity, 110, 124
interference, 108
interferon, 67
Internal Revenue Service, 124
investment, 110
issues, viii, 2, 4, 27

J

jurisdiction, 86

K

kidney, ix, 6, 51, 52, 53, 56, 57, 58, 60, 61, 62, 63, 66, 73, 74, 75, 79, 81, 83, 90, 96, 121
kidney failure, ix, 6, 83
kidney XE "kidney" transplantation, 121

L

labeling, 81
laboratory tests, 96, 100
laws, 87, 88, 124
lead, 106
legislation, 6, 13, 20, 25, 35, 88, 89, 100
legislative authority, 29, 30, 31
legs, 101

leukemia, 68, 69
life expectancy, 94
lifetime, 93, 118
light, 124
local community, 120
local government, 12, 43
long-term services, 18
long-term services and supports, 18
long-term services and supports (LTSS), 18
lower prices, 49
LTC, 117
lung disease, 57, 61, 74, 90
lymphoma, 68

M

macular degeneration, 50, 51, 52, 53, 58, 59, 75
majority, 7, 18, 36, 48, 56, 74, 115
malignancy, 68
management, 94
marketing, 49, 50, 51, 69, 81
marriage, 16
married couples, 24
Maryland, 122
matter, iv
median, 100, 103
Medicaid, viii, ix, 2, 3, 7, 11, 17, 18, 19, 20, 21, 22, 23, 26, 27, 31, 33, 34, 37, 38, 39, 40, 41, 43, 46, 47, 49, 83, 84, 87, 88, 107, 108, 111, 114, 115, 116, 117, 121, 122, 124, 125
medical, vii, 1, 3, 41, 46, 80, 87, 93, 94, 95, 96, 97, 98, 101, 103, 104, 105, 119, 122
medical care, 95, 105
Medicare Modernization Act, 14
Medicare Part A, vii, 1, 4, 10, 36, 43, 80, 87, 104, 112, 113, 117
medicine, 98
meningitis, 52, 53, 61, 76
mental health, 93, 98, 122
mesothelioma, 67
metastatic disease, 68
methodology, 13, 122
metropolitan areas, 101
microorganisms, 80
military, viii, 1, 8, 9, 25, 115
MMA, 14, 28, 30, 31, 40, 43, 88, 100, 101, 108, 109, 110, 115, 117, 123
models, 43, 111
modifications, viii, x, 2, 84, 87, 88
multiple myeloma, 68, 69
muscle strength, 69
myelodysplastic syndromes, 69

N

National Defense Authorization Act, 9
National Institutes of Health, 46
natural disaster, 16
nausea, 53, 59, 77
neuropathy, 60, 69, 79
neutral, 122
neutropenia, 61, 68, 76
non-Hodgkin's lymphoma, 50
nurses, 104
nursing, ix, 3, 83, 85, 92, 94, 95, 99, 104, 110, 122, 123
nursing care, 85, 95
nursing home, 110, 122
nutrition, 104

O

obesity, 100
obstacles, 104
occupational therapy, 95, 99
Office of Management and Budget, 117
Office of the Inspector General, 123
officials, 47
OMB, 117, 121
operations, 109, 111
organ, 57, 59, 61, 68, 74, 75, 101, 102

osteoarthritis, 52
osteoporosis, 48, 55, 100
outpatient, vii, viii, 1, 3, 37, 41, 45, 46, 47, 48, 49, 80, 81, 85, 88, 97, 98, 99, 100, 102, 103, 107, 118, 122
outpatients, 80, 102
outreach, 109
oversight, ix, 84, 86
oxygen, 101

P

palliative, 94
parity, 122
participants, viii, 2, 11
pathology, 95, 99
payroll, vii, 1, 2, 3, 4, 43, 85, 87, 90, 111, 112
pegfilgrastim, 51, 61
penalties, 4, 5, 10, 14, 25, 37
per capita cost, 6, 13, 16, 24, 38
perfusion, 53, 60, 75
permission, iv
permit, 102
pharmaceuticals, 102
physical therapist, 99
physical therapy, 99
physicians, viii, 14, 45, 49, 50, 87, 97, 98, 99, 102, 103, 104, 120
platinum, 68
pneumonia, 52, 53, 56, 61, 76
podiatrists, 98
policy, 26, 28, 29, 30, 31, 49, 80, 103
population, 2, 7, 8, 20, 25, 46, 47, 48, 57, 58, 74, 75, 76, 77, 78, 79, 81, 85, 97, 114
population group, 20, 25
poverty, 18, 19, 20, 41, 108, 125
preparation, iv
prescription drugs, ix, 3, 80, 83, 102, 107
President, 26, 27, 43
prevention, 52, 53, 61, 76, 100, 123
price changes, 56
private information, 110
private practice, 99
private sector, 88, 110
professionals, 99, 102, 104
project, 47
protection, 20, 114
public assistance, 11
public health, 90
Puerto Rico, 37, 110
pulmonary arteries, 54
pulmonary hypertension, 54
purchasing power, 20
purity, 81

Q

quality assurance, 110
quality improvement, 106, 111
quality standards, 110

R

race, 97
radiation, 68
radiation therapy, 68
radioisotope, 101
radium, 101
radius, 104
recommendations, iv, 89
reconciliation, 88
recovery, 102, 103
red blood cells, 80
reform, x, 84, 86, 88, 109
rehabilitation, 94, 99
reimbursements, ix, 84, 99
rejection, 57, 59, 61, 68, 74, 75
reliability, 47
remission, 67
renal cell carcinoma, 67
requirements, 26, 41, 99, 104, 107, 120, 122, 125
resource utilization, 94

resources, 4, 18, 19, 89, 122
response, 67, 86, 87
restrictions, 105
restructuring, 86
retail, 101
retirement, 3, 4, 9, 11, 12, 37
revenue, 13, 14, 42, 88, 111
rheumatoid arthritis, 50, 51, 52, 62, 76
rights, iv
risk, 69, 100, 105, 108
rituximab, 67
rules, 18, 38, 40, 87, 88, 89, 103, 109, 121
rural areas, 96

S

safety, 39, 81, 110
savings, 19, 40, 89, 105
savings account, 19
sclerosis, 62, 79
scope, 80, 115
Secretary of Defense, 10
securities, 111, 112
self-employed, 112
Senate, 45, 86
services, iv, vii, ix, 1, 2, 3, 13, 18, 19, 24, 26, 43, 80, 81, 83, 84, 85, 87, 88, 89, 92, 93, 94, 95, 96, 97, 98, 99, 100, 101, 102, 103, 104, 105, 110, 111, 113, 114, 115, 122, 123
shingles, 80
shortage, 104
shortness of breath, 57, 61, 74
showing, 48
side effects, 51, 56
signs, 5, 44, 67
SNP, 118
social security, 112
Social Security, viii, ix, 2, 3, 4, 10, 11, 12, 15, 16, 18, 19, 20, 21, 22, 23, 24, 28, 29, 33, 37, 38, 39, 40, 41, 42, 43, 83, 84, 87, 90, 112, 113, 118, 121, 123, 124, 125
Social Security Administration, 4, 10, 20, 39, 42
Social Security beneficiaries, viii, 2, 11, 22, 24
Social Security Disability Insurance, 38, 121
social services, 95
social workers, 98
sodium, 60
specialists, 105
speech, 95, 99
spending, viii, ix, 2, 12, 20, 24, 26, 27, 46, 48, 50, 56, 80, 84, 85, 86, 87, 88, 89, 90, 98, 106, 107, 111, 113, 114, 120, 121, 123, 125
squamous cell, 68
squamous cell carcinoma, 68
SSA, 5, 10, 29, 38, 39, 40, 41, 42, 118
SSI, 118
stakeholders, 85
standard of living, 24
state, 11, 12, 18, 20, 41, 43, 85, 87, 104, 110, 115, 122, 125
states, viii, 19, 41, 45, 106, 110, 112, 114, 115
stress, 52
stress test, 52
structure, 86, 89
Subsidies, 41
subsidy, 27, 41, 43, 89, 92, 108, 120, 123
sucrose, 62
supervision, viii, 45, 48
supplier, 101, 104, 109
suppliers, 110, 121, 122
support services, 94
sustainable growth, 14, 98
symptoms, 67, 69
syndrome, 52, 54, 58, 59, 62, 68, 75, 78
synthesis, 62, 78

T

target, 98
Task Force, 100, 118, 123
taxes, vii, 1, 2, 3, 4, 44, 87, 90, 111, 112
technical comments, 56
techniques, 105, 111
technologies, 93, 102, 110
technology, 14, 102
terminal illness, 94
testing, 81, 88
therapy, 67, 68, 69, 95, 99, 100, 101, 102, 104, 122
thrombocytopenia, 68
thrombocytopenic purpura, 61, 77
tissue, 103
total costs, 13
tracks, 41
trade, 15
training, 104
transfer of money, 111
transfer payments, 41, 85
transformation, 68, 69
transplant, ix, 49, 57, 59, 61, 74, 75, 83, 90, 102
transplantation, 96
transport, 123
transportation, 104
Treasury, 3, 13, 14, 111, 113
treatment, 6, 50, 53, 55, 61, 67, 68, 69, 76, 81, 93, 94, 96, 99, 102
trial, 50
trust fund, ix, 3, 13, 14, 20, 42, 43, 84, 85, 87, 109, 111, 112, 113, 114
Trust Fund, 3, 23, 31, 36, 42, 43, 122, 124, 125
tumors, 54

U

U.S. Treasury, 111
ulcerative colitis, 67
unions, 43, 108
United, v, ix, 4, 10, 43, 45, 46, 48, 49, 80, 83, 118
United States, v, ix, 4, 10, 43, 45, 46, 48, 49, 80, 83, 118
updating, 29
urban, 18, 94, 95
urinalysis, 100

V

vaccine, 56, 61, 62, 80, 100
variations, 13, 98, 107
vasoactive intestinal peptide, 54, 62, 77
Volunteers, 10
vomiting, 53, 59, 77

W

wage level, 95
wages, 42, 94, 96
Washington, 45
waste, 109
web, 38
welfare, 87
wheezing, 57, 61, 74
wholesale, 49
workers, viii, 2, 3, 9, 12, 39, 85, 87, 91, 111